# WILLETTA GREENE  JOHNSON, PH. D.

# GLORY RISING

## How the Glory of God
## Shapes Your Destiny in Today's World

**Willetta Greene Johnson, Ph.D.**
smuinc@gmail.com

ISBN-13: 978-1-51718-430-8
ISBN-10: 1517184304
Copyright © 2015
Printed in the United States

**Edited by:**
Julie P. Gordon

**Cover and Interior Design:**
Master's Touch Graphics
Minnie Watkins
masterstouchgraphics.com

---

This book is dedicated to my dear friend and fellow psalmist Lenora Woods. She has consistently radiated joy and generosity all the years I've known her. Through her walk with Christ, I see the testimony of Glory rising. In spite of her most intense battles, she is a worshipper, an encourager, and a *more than conqueror*.

---

# TABLE OF CONTENT

# ABOUT THE AUTHOR

Willetta Greene Johnson, Ph. D., is a physicist, professional producer, Grammy award songwriter, and author. She received her classical piano training from Dr. Irene Rosenberg Grau. She received her degrees in physics from Stanford University (B. S.) and from the University of Chicago, specializing in theoretical statistical mechanics and surface spectroscopy. Dr. Greene Johnson is currently Senior Lecturer in the College of Arts and Sciences and a Master Teacher in physics and chemistry at Loyola University Chicago.

A sought-after consultant, speaker, worship leader and clinician, Dr. Greene Johnson's expertise spans from encompassing the physical sciences and science education to reconciliation, worship, integrity and team-building to orchestration, branding, coaching, studio and live production. Her unique journey places her at the interesting intersection of science and faith, art and intellect, empathy versus economy, left brain versus right brain.

Dr. Greene Johnson has received numerous awards in teaching excellence, community leadership and the music industry. In 2004, her song Saved was graced to be part of the Grammy-winning project, *Live: This is Your House* recorded by The Brooklyn Tabernacle Choir Her works have been performed or premiered by the Chicago Sinfonietta Orchestra, the Memphis Symphony Orchestra, Old St. Patrick Catholic Church (Chicago), the Brooklyn Tabernacle Choir, Fellowship MB Church, Mary Mary, and notable others.

Dr. Greene-Johnson has been married for 30 years to Arnold Johnson Jr., an image stylist, colorist, and hair salon owner. They have one son who is currently pursuing a master's degree in political science.

*Mine eyes have seen the coming*
*of the glory of the Lord.*
Battle Hymn of the Republic
Julia W. Howe  (1861)

# 1

# WHAT IS GLORY?

*Arise, shine, for your light has come and the Glory of
the Lord rises upon you.  Is. 60:1 (NIV)*

If on some occasion you have attended an African American
church, you may have heard the refrain:

> *I come to glorify His Name*
> *I come to glorify His Name*
> *I come to glorify the Name of the Lord*
> *Glorify His Name.*

And one can't forget the beloved refrain from the Battle Hymn of
the Republic

> *Glory Glory Hallelujah*
> *Glory Glory Hallelujah*
> *Glory Glory Hallelujah*
> *His Truth is marching on!*

But—what does the invocation, 'Glory!' mean? What does
glorifying the Lord mean? Answer: to give God glory.  Fantastic,
now, what does it mean to give God glory? If all the glory belongs
to God, then how can *we* give God glory?

Even more basic than that, *what is Glory?*

Many believers really don't know what Glory is. They may think
it is power, or light; something that occurs mainly in heaven or at
Christmas time. To some of you, Glory may be a vague concept.
So if we don't know what Glory is, how can we give it to God?

How do we even know that we gave it correctly?

In Jesus' profound prayer in John 17, He indicated that the Glory God gave Him, He in turn had given to His disciples (Jn. 17:22). According to Jesus, we who are born again have received the Glory of God inside of us. How do we tap into it? What are we supposed to be doing with it?

Finally, consider the riveting events happening in our earth today. It seems as if the world has gone berserk. Wars and rumor of more wars, birds dropping dead from the sky, increased violence and mean spiritedness, unpredictable and damaging weather, terror and cyber coordinated terrorism. There's some tragedy in every news cycle for which one shakes one's head.[1]

What in the world is going on?

Answer: **Glory**. God's glory is on the rise. God's glory has moved 'one inch' closer to earth. All of the events we listed relate to this very Glory we're about to converse about. More precisely, they are examples of the world system's failure and demise in the presence of Glory.

And let me give you a spoiler alert: that bold assignment that God has laid on your heart to accomplish? You're going to need God's glory richly operating in your life to get it done.

The same Glory that is shaking down the world is shaping up God's people. The same Glory that exposes the inferiority and utter failure of worldly logic reveals the superiority and excellency of God's wisdom. The same Glory that, by its very purity, wreaks havoc in the perverse world system provides the power and resources through which your destiny in Christ will come to pass.

In fact, this current turbulent, indeed dangerous time is the greatest of times for the saints to walk in the Glory of God. You are part of that blessed generation of believers that will boldly arise and shine in Jesus' Name! Isaiah 60:1 exhorts us:

*Arise, shine, for your light has come and the glory of the Lord rises upon you. (NIV)*

So don't be afraid when you hear an unsettling news broadcast; Jesus told us to fear none of these things. The Glory of God is your protector and the lifter of your head (Ps. 3:3). And precisely because we are in the last days, because of the escalation of world events swirling about us, it is beneficial to better understand what Glory is.

So as you read the words in this book, I pray that the mercy and love of God saturate you and minister to you. I pray that this book helps you to:

- understand the preeminent and pivotal role of God's glory in your life;
- recognize the move of Glory in the world;
- appreciate the tremendous opportunities to evangelize and demonstrate God's love; and, most of all
- convince somebody to receive the Lord Jesus Christ and be gloriously saved.

**So let's dive in.**

The word 'glory' occurs 402 times in 371 verses in forty-eight of the 66 books of the Bible spanning from Genesis to Revelations.[2] In the Old Testament, the most prominent Hebrew word translated 'glory' is *kabod* and in the New Testament, the most prominent Greek word is *doxa* (δοξα). In fact, a doxology, such as the one at the end of the Lord's prayer—

*For Thine is the kingdom, the power, and the glory, forever, Amen.*

—literally means *praise* or *glory speaking*.

The last time you opened your mouth, was that glory speaking?

The English word 'glory' derives from its Latin origin, *gloria,* which means *fame, renown.* But in the Bible, glory does not just indicate fame, or "rock-star" status. When describing God's glory, it conveys infinitely more significance than merely reputation.

So, before we can begin to appreciate how the glory of God is so vital and so impactful in our lives, we need to define the glory of God. Just what is the glory of God? It is safe to say that one could spend a lifetime just trying to articulate the nonpareil significance of God's glory in the entire universe and still not have scratched the surface. But this book serves as just a primer, so a practical working definition will suffice. We need to start somewhere, and trust that God will meet us where we are.

*The glory of God is His character, the essence of Who God is.* This statement is both simple and profound at the same time. As it relates to us, the glory of God is the manifestation and revelation of God's love to us.[3]

However, this revelation is not just a ploy to entertain or amaze the viewer. It is not like the revealing of a new tech gadget (think iPhone), or a new concert tour or a more astounding daredevil feat. Biblical revelation is not an exhibition that simply thrills and wows the audience.

*In Christ, revelation produces transformation.*

Another point: *the glory of God is territorial.* Similar to light (electromagnetic radiation) Glory shines forth, expands, permeates, fills a space and banishes the darkness that previously occupied that space. Light, not darkness sets the agenda. As with light, the influence or "reach" of Glory increases with its intensity. Just as headlights set to high beam can pierce more darkness than the low beam setting,

**The more Glory, the more territory.**

So when Glory shows up, it's overwhelming. I'm not talking about people enjoyed the service. I'm talking about people floored in the service. God is omnipotent: His presence is POTENT.

When God's glory manifests—when 'God shows up'—it's concentrated, heavy, not the normal air that we breathe. When God's glory is manifested, His *omnipresence* becomes *very present* (Ps. 46:1). It's a holy atmosphere full of mercy and goodness and love that we just inhale, we just breathe in.

*In Him we move, we breathe, and have our being…*

So the glory of God is a potent defining revelation of God's love that progressively transforms us to be more like God![4] A quick way to remember it:

> **G**od's
> **L**ove
> **O**verflows
> **R**estoring
> **Y**ou

or more bluntly:

> **G**od's
> **L**ove
> **O**ver
> **R**ules
> **Y**ou

Notice the word 'over' in both of these acronyms. God's glory is manifested when there's an *overflow*. Not a little bit, rather an overflow. God's love overflowing brings restoration. God's glory is manifest when your ambition is over-ruled. Notice that both acronyms start with 'God' and end with 'you'. God is first and you are last. God's plan over-rules yours. And my friend, achieving that hierarchy is no small feat. That is the *crux*, literally the *cross* we must bear, of Christian maturity, for growing up in Christ absolutely requires crucifying our own agenda.

**Give God Great Glory**. As believers, however, we cannot let the matter rest at *defining* God's glory. Jesus died on Calvary's Cross to redeem us; He bore the horrid punishment for our sins that we deserved. We cannot simply admire from a distance God's character, how good and loving and powerful God is. We cannot be merely spectators on the sidelines. God doesn't seek fans. He seeks players in the game who, through Christ, become game-changers. He seeks disciples, those who will allow the Holy Spirit to discipline and radically alter their lives.

> God so loved that He gave.
> We must be so grateful that we reciprocate.

We must resolve to conduct our lives in a way that gives God glory. (When we speak of men giving glory to God the word *glory* is better interpreted as *honor*.) And because the precious gift of salvation was procured so freely for us at so great a price to Jesus, we must strive to *give God great glory*. But just what does that mean? How does one 'bless the Lord at all times'? How does one magnify the Lord? How does one give God great glory?

The amazing response is that we cannot do so without God's glory ruling our lives, starting with salvation. *God must equip us by His Spirit to give Him glory.*

2 Corinthians 3:18 says: *But we all, with open face beholding as in a glass (mirror) the glory of the Lord, are changed into the same image from glory to glory, even as by the Spirit of the Lord.* — The word 'behold' in that verse is akin to meditation, keeping a steady gaze.

As we steadily gaze upon God's Word with open face and an open heart, we are changed into the very attribute upon which we meditate. Not all at once, but progressively we are transformed from glory to glory by intensely focusing upon the Word of God.

It's miraculous that—via this reverential gazing into the transparent mirror of God's Word—we are transformed into His likeness. Supernaturally we evolve from giving God glory to giving God greater glory. We are translated from our present ability to obey God to an increased ability to obey God. This wondrous process will be detailed in a later chapter.

Romans 8:30 concludes with 'whom that He justified, them He also glorified'. The process described in 2 Corinthians 3:18 must be what is meant by *glorification*—increasing from glory to glory.

Glorification, then, is the miraculous and continual renewal of our minds. And as it is God who instituted glorification through the finished work of Calvary, it must give God glory and delight for His children to mature from glory to glory. This makes understanding how to give God great glory all the more imperative!

These are the lessons that we must learn. Now that we are equipped with a definition, namely, the glory of God speaks to His character, and now that we are charged with a hallowed, sacred vocation to give God great glory, here are some important questions that this book will endeavor to answer.

- How does God's glory impact who I can become?
- How does the glory of God or its absence affect the earth?
- How is there a correlation between God's glory and current world events?
- How can the glory of God heal my pain and correct my past?
- How can my life give God great glory?

There is only one action point I request of you: that you read the pages of this book in earnest expectation of being transformed by the *scriptures* throughout the book that are impressed upon you by the Holy Spirit. This book is incapable of changing you. But pursuing the scriptures in this book that leap out at you and *meditating upon those scriptures will transform you*.

As you read in expectation of being transformed, I pray that the Lord highlights the words that will empower and transform you. I pray that these words impart *doxa*, glory into your life, by which is meant, more of God's character, His love, His strength, His mercy and grace, and the direction He has for your life.

I pray that you become a powerful and stunning representative of God's glory.

Your unique walk with God and adventures in Christ will refine and improve upon the definition of Glory that has been provided; it's just a beginning attempt to characterize the glory of God. As you continue to walk with God, the full revelation of the magnificence of God's glory will be tailored just for you.

# CHAPTER
# 2

## GLORY IN CREATION

*For by him were all things created, that are in heaven, and that are in earth, visible and invisible, whether they be thrones, or dominions, or principalities, or powers: all things were created by him, and for him: And he is before all things, and by him all things consist.*
*Col. 1:16,17 (KJV)*

The essence of who God is, and thus, the essence of His Glory certainly includes His unique role as Creator. The name of God that emphasizes this creative attribute is *Elohim* and it is used in Genesis 1:1:

*In the beginning, Elohim created the heavens and the earth.*

The words of God are creative and substantive. His words evoke a life force that produces a specific outcome. They do not suggest; they command. God spoke the universe into existence. This is substantiated by Hebrews 11:3, which declares:

*Through faith we understand that the worlds were framed by the word of God, so that things which are seen were not made of things which do appear. (KJV)*

Another translation says: *By faith we understand that the entire universe was formed at God's command, that what we now see did not come from anything that can be seen. (NLT)*

The Words of God provided everything that was needed to create the specific outcome. The void, the emptiness to which the Lord spoke, didn't have to supply anything. In fact it was incapable of doing so. When God spoke 'Let there be light', the void didn't have to know what light was. **Whatever light is, it completely came from God**. This is an important concept. The signature of a Glory action, a God-assignment: it requires *absolutely no assistance* from the recipient.

God's creation—planets, stars, galaxies—testifies of Him, and the order of the cosmos proclaims God's excellence and majesty, endless resources, as well as His staggering and infinite wisdom. Every thing that God has created testifies of Him (or will one day). According to Psalm 19, the heavens and the sky above declare God's glory and exemplify Who God is. Every discipline reinforces that He exists and that He reigns.

*The heavens declare the glory of God; and the firmament sheweth his handywork. ²Day unto day uttereth speech, and night unto night sheweth knowledge. ³There is no speech nor language, where their voice is not heard. Ps. 19:1-3 (KJV)*

Whether mathematics or law, botany or weaving, theology or football, physics or music, there is no discipline where the *logos*— the *logic* of God is not manifest.[5] There is no discipline where we do not see His beauty, the excellency of His wisdom, His penchant for symmetry and order, His love for radiance and life. Recalling that our definition of the glory of God is the essence of who He is, the qualities just described certainly comprise His glory.

The main part of our glory journey will revolve around the relation between God and His child. However, the staging for the realization of that remarkable collaboration occurred way before humankind arrived on the scene. God was thinking about you and me even before the earth was created. Ephesians 1:4 reveals:

*Even before he made the world, God loved us and chose us in Christ to be holy and without fault in his eyes. (NLT)*

*According as he hath chosen us in him before the foundation of the world, that we should be holy and without blame before him in love: (KJV)*

Before the foundation of the world was established, God had thought about you and had determined to choose you, *which immediately established your significance and worth* in His divine plan.

You have great significance. You have purpose. God has a wonderful plan for your life. We need your gifts to be fully developed. We need what God has called you to do.[6] You are indeed fearfully and wondrously made, so give God glory for your very existence! (Ps. 139:14)

You see, to really comprehend the quality of relationship God desires with you and me and the role that Glory plays in it, we have to go back—not only before the creation of man, but before there was even a universe, to when there was only God and His thoughts. If we want to understand our spiritual genome, how we are coded to interact in and respond to God's glory, we have to travel back to the proto-beginning, before the foundation of the world.

It's imperative for you to know how secure you are in Jesus. Before you were created, before your parents were created, before the stars were created, God saw *you*. He had thoughts about *you* (Jer. 29:11): your freckles, or dimples. The shape of your nose. The color of your eyes. Your laugh. Your gifts and talents. How those gifts were layered, when and under what circumstances they would be unwrapped. Your hopes and fears, strengths and weaknesses. Elohim God saw this for each and every person He intended to create.

God also foresaw that the fallen angel satan, who had been cast out of heaven, unable to contend with God, would execute full vengeance and spite upon humans. Introducing self-ambition and disloyalty, satan would successfully deceive mankind and cause them to violate the holy ordinance and sacred trust.

God, being utterly holy and righteous, knew that this rebellion had to be judged. The very essence of His universe was designed in divine order and for divine purpose, so ultimately acts of rebellion, *i.e.*, sin had to be destroyed.

In a later chapter we will see scriptures indicating that when there is too much sin in the land, too much 'sin per square acre', or when sin has infected an area longer than the God-appointed grace period, the earth *is designed* to react in a way that evicts the cause of the sin. The universe, by the purposed design of its Creator, will not indefinitely support the enterprise of sin.

So God foresaw that man would sin, and fall from the glory of God. But God *so* loved that He did not want the human race to be destroyed by sin. So—get this, really get this—even before we messed up, God had devised a plan. God determined to provide a Lamb to take away the sins of the world (1 Pet. 1:20).

This monumental decision of extraordinary mercy and amazing grace is captured in Psalm 40:7,8 where Jesus announces His willingness to carry out the mission of salvation.

*⁷ Then said I, Lo, I come: in the volume of the book it is written of me, ⁸ I delight to do thy will, O my God: yea, thy law is within my heart. (KJV)*

Hebrews 10:5-7 confirms that the passage in Psalm 40 refers to Christ:

*⁵Therefore, when Christ came into the world, he said: "Sacrifice and offering you did not desire, but a body you prepared for me; ⁶ with burnt offerings and sin offerings you were not pleased. ⁷ Then I said, 'Here I am—it is written about me in the scroll—I have come to do your will, my God' (NIV)*

1 Peter 1:20 clearly states: *'He (Christ) was chosen before the creation of the world, but was revealed in these last times for your sake.' (NIV)*

Through these magnanimous acts, we learn more of God's character, and therefore gaze more intently upon the glory of God. What have we learned?

Our God is a God who does all things well. He leaves nothing to chance. His Will gets done. Yes, mankind would fall and fail, but Christ would prevail and, through salvation, God would reinstate His children to be with Him—legitimately, justifiably—forever.

And it is also equally amazing that God had so much faith in His process, He had so much faith in His love that, even though mankind would rebel against Him, love would win in the end. Even though by God's own decree, Adam and Eve, having fallen from grace, would reproduce after their kind—insuring that the blight of sin was passed from one generation to the next—God staked the full success of His plan of redemption on His only begotten Son, Jesus.

God was exceedingly confident that Jesus, Son of God and Son of man, born of a woman, born in flesh capable of sin, surrounded by temptation, would overcome all temptation and *impeccably* carry out the mission of ultimate sacrifice—death on Calvary's Cross for the sins of the entire world. God was abundantly confident love would over-rule and more than conquer in the end.

God really *believes* that love never fails.

And so should we! God is love. He never fails. It follows that any strategy of love with pure motive born of God will never, ever fail.[7]

# WHAT THE HEAVENS TEACH US ABOUT GOD'S GLORY

*The heavens declare the glory of God; the skies proclaim the work of His hands. Ps. 19:1 (NIV)*

What does the glory in the cosmos teach us about the glory of God, or about our relation with Him? What can we learn from that celestial tapestry? The Bible assures us in Psalm 19:3 that there is no speech or language wherein the voice of God is not heard. So, when we look up at the stars, when we consider the heavenly bodies that reside there, as well as some extraordinary discoveries that scientists have observed, what does God's voice say to us?

It turns out that we may learn several principles.

(1) **The heavens provide a scale by which we can compare our small selves**. Understanding our utter dependence upon God is wisdom we should treasure. There are few experiences more humbling than a good look at the heavens. Just the size of objects such as stars, galaxies, nebulae, black holes, as well as the number of them staggers the imagination.

For instance, our Sun occupies a million times more volume than the earth but the red giant star Betelguese, located in the constellation Orion, occupies a million times more volume than our *Sun* (trillion times more than Earth). Betelguese is so huge that if it replaced our Sun at the center of the solar system, its surface would intercept Jupiter. (Mercury, Venus, Earth and Mars would be swallowed).[8]

And this is but one fascinating star in the vast tapestry of the heavens!

Psalm 8:3-4 says *When I consider thy heavens, the work of thy fingers, the moon and the stars, which thou hast ordained, what is man that You are mindful of Him or the son of man that You visit him? (NKJV)*

Indeed, compared to God, His glory, His grandeur, His galaxies, what is man?

Recognizing *smallness* doesn't lower *self-esteem*. We are made in the image of God. He has placed eternity in our hearts—a beacon by which to draw us nearer to Himself, and we are fearfully and wonderfully made.[9] But we were created to be the junior partner in God's collaborations, and this point must never be forgotten.

Bad decisions are made when humans overestimate their abilities or resources. Paul admonished believers to not over-rate themselves, but have a balanced, honest self-assessment (Rom.12:3). Overestimation leads to misdirected ambition—that is what got Adam and Eve in trouble from the start.

Recognizing our vulnerability and frailty motivates us to trust in God, to lean only on Him. Adam and Eve got fooled into thinking that the Lord was keeping something good from them. Unfortunately, they did not question the vile source; instead they leaned on their own understanding and questioned God's goodwill.

They were utterly mistaken: in the presence of God they were *surrounded* by goodness and mercy. Everything that the Lord taught them was good. The only new thing the Adams learned by eating the forbidden fruit was *evil*. Tragically, that one action caused them to fall from grace, cost them access to God's presence, and ultimately cost their lives.

Let us resolve to learn from the heavens and lean on the Lord. It is an excellent practice each day to thank the Lord for being mindful of us, and then, in turn, be mindful to follow His instructions, our daily bread.[10]

**(2) The heavens provide a dynamic visual aid to comprehend a limitless God**. Teachers often use visual aids to get a point across. Well, when God revealed His plan to give Abraham a son in his old age, God—Master Teacher that He is—invited Abraham to look up at the stars and try to count them.

God told Abraham in Gen. 15:5, paraphrased, *Look up towards heaven and count the stars, if you are able to. So shall your seed be!* When God calls a man or a woman to greatness, to manifest the greatness that is already in them, He always invites them to look up to heaven.

*...Look up, and lift up your heads, because your redemption draws nigh. Lk. 21:28 (KJV)*

*Set your mind on things above, not on things on the earth. Col. 3:2 (NKJV)*

There are at least 100 million galaxies in the observable universe. If you held up one grain of sand, the patch of sky it covers contains ten thousand galaxies.[11] Each galaxy contains about 100 billion stars. Our Sun is but one of those hundred billion stars in our galaxy the Milky Way.

There exists, conservatively, 10 billion trillion stars in the universe.[12] I must admit that it's hard for me to wrap my mind around that number. I can write it in scientific notation, but it doesn't process like the number one billion (population of India, and of China). I don't live day-to-day dealing with numbers like $10^{24}$. Neither does the billionaire!

The number of stars is so gargantuan, it might as well be infinity. Yet Psalm 147:4 says that *our God knows each one by name*. So the scale that God lives in, and the wisdom that He evokes literally dwarfs one's biggest expectations. What this great God of glory has already done, and what He desires to accomplish in you *exceeds* abundantly above (Eph. 3:20).

**(3) The vastness of the heavens challenges us to expand our faith**. God desires for you to sit with Christ in heavenly places (Eph. 2:6). But it's not so we can claim boasting rights. We must still be yielded to Jesus. It's not enough to be a Christian touting faith, faith to believe for this, faith to believe for that, but it's time to have faith to obey the hard things that God desires us to do.

Having faith pleases God, but it's not ours to direct as *we* please. God has not called us to faith. He *gave* us the measure of faith. Rather, God has called us to *faithfulness*. He desires us to be so full, so faithful, so obedient that we will not manipulate and abuse our privileges in Christ, we will only execute Kingdom mandates. It's time to be full of faith that gives glory to God (Rom. 4:20). It's time to develop a faith that carries out a God-assignment *to completion*. And that requires an expansion of our capacity to believe.

When God first told Abraham (then Abram) that he was going to have a son, he was 90 years old and his wife Sarah was 75 years old. They had not been spring chickens for a while. For Abraham and Sarah to believe that God could give them a biological son required a radical expansion of their capacity to believe. You've got to see in your mind's eye a God so huge, so able, so generous, so unlimited—that impossible *itself* becomes a non-option.

And here's the other thing you need to know about a God-assignment: God's not about to assign you *anything* that's possible for you to do on your own. Because then, He wouldn't get all the glory.[13]

So, beloved, in order to realize that promise, that bold project that God showed you, you're going to have to pray and fast and read your Bible. You're going to have to partner with the God of all excellent possibilities—on His terms—to realize your humanly impossible assignment and get your victory.

**(4) There is order in the cosmos**. The moon revolves around the earth; the earth revolves around the sun. Our solar system revolves about the Galactic Center of the Milky Way which itself speeds along through the universe at approximately one million miles per hour.[14] *Every heavenly body stays in its lane*. Permanently. Every *HEAVENLY* body stays in its lane. Planets and stars do not rebel. There is order in the cosmos.

This would be a powerful principle to practice in our churches. Lord, help us to actively seek unity in Christ and to get along kindly with each other. Let us check ambition and competition and just stay in our lane. Let us cease from fretting and scheming, causing friction, creating more heat than light in the process. The Apostle Paul appealed for unity in the Body of Christ in Ephesians Chapter 4:

[14]*That we henceforth be no more children, tossed to and fro, and carried about with every wind of doctrine, by the sleight of men, and cunning craftiness, whereby they lie in wait to deceive;*
[15]*But speaking the truth in love, may grow up into him in all things, which is the head, even Christ:*
[16]*From whom the whole body fitly joined together and compacted by that which every joint supplieth, according to the effectual working in the measure of every part, maketh increase of the body unto the edifying of itself in love. Eph. 4:14-16 (KJV)*

The orderly courses of the sun, moon, and stars declare that God is glorious. Let us not be bested by stars and planets. If inanimate objects in the heavens can run like clockwork, surely the Church, the redeemed of the Lord can strive for effectiveness, harmony and goodwill as together we serve Christ. This is an essential way to bless the Lord and give God even greater glory.

**(5) In the universe, stationary doesn't mean stagnant**. Our universe is expanding. It is in continuous transformation. Nothing is stagnant or sitting still. Entire galaxies are racing through space at amazing speeds. New stars are constantly being birthed even as ancient stars burst into spectacular supernovae. At this moment, though you may be sitting in one place, you're rotating around the center of the Earth at a rate approximately 1000 miles per hour, which itself revolves about the Sun at 67,000 miles per hour. Being still certainly doesn't mean going nowhere in this case!

Nor is it the case spiritually when it feels as though the 'pause button' has been pressed in your life. Just because you appear to be in a holding pattern doesn't mean that progress is not being made. If you remain faithful to God's plan, your life is being transformed for the better, even though you may not sense it yet.

Moreover, God desires that we appreciate resting in Him. There is purpose in rest. In fact, rest belongs to God and only He can give it. We don't get rest from vacations. We get *temporary relief* from vacations. We get rest from God. In Hebrews, we find that God determines who may or may not enter into His rest.

*So I sware in my wrath, They shall not enter into my rest.  Heb. 3:11 (KJV)*

*[9]There remaineth therefore a rest to the people of God. [10]For he that is entered into his rest, he also hath ceased from his own works, as God did from his. [11]Let us labour therefore to enter into that rest, lest any man fall after the same example of unbelief.  Heb. 4:9-11 (KJV)*

Recall one of the acronyms for 'glory' from Chapter 1,

God's
**Love**
Over
Rules
You

One of the ways that God's love *rules over* us is when we drop the 'busy bee' routine. We cease from fretting, we cease from micromanaging our own lives. We let go, and let God, and just relax in the love of God. If God knows all of the stars, all ten billion trillion of them *by name,*[15] He's *got* this. Chill.

**(6) The universe consists mostly of energy derived from sources we cannot see.** Our universe is a gargantuan producer of energy in forms including light and heat that is constantly being transferred and shared with lesser bodies. For instance, the Earth receives its energy, and maintains its ambient temperature of about 70 degrees Fahrenheit (25 degrees Celsius) from Sun energy. However, here's another amazing fact about the distribution of power (rate of energy production) in the universe.

Scientists have discovered that the greatest sources of energy in our universe are found in so-called *dark matter* and *dark energy.* In fact, nearly 96% of all energy in the universe is NOT due to atoms, to ordinary material.[16] It's due to stuff we can't even see. It resides in a substance that hasn't yet been identified. In other words, most of the energy sustaining the activities of the universe—keeping the whole thing going—*is derived from sources that are not seen.*

What spiritual lesson do we gain from this amazing astronomical discovery, that most of the power in the physical universe comes from sources that you can't observe? It brings to mind Hebrews 11:3, which bluntly declares: *Through faith we understand that the worlds were framed by the word of God, so that things which are seen were not made of things which do appear. (KJV)*

Think about it! 96% of the energy in this universe is not due to nuclear explosions, fusion, and conventional forms of energy. It's due to power sources we can't even see. Doesn't that sound familiar? And given Who created the universe, is it even surprising? Proverbs 25:2 says: *the glory of God is to conceal a thing but the honor of kings is to search a matter out. (KJV)*

We believers in Christ also have hidden power, power hidden in earthly vessels *that the excellency may be of God and not of ourselves* (2 Cor. 4:18).

The greatest source of power comes from the faithfulness you can't see. It comes from the prayers and intercessions no one else hears. It comes from your integrity that no one else seems to even appreciate. But, thanks be to God, the God of glory hears your prayers and your intercessions, He sees your integrity, and He will richly reward you and all His faithful children.

In conclusion, dear one, God uses the sky as His celestial blackboard to teach us about Himself. When we look up at the night sky, and consider the heavens,

- we see light
- we see order
- we see direction
- we see vastness
- we see constancy and faithfulness

In short, we are precisely describing the glory of God.

# 4

# FALL FROM GLORY

*For all have sinned and fall short of the glory of God…*
*Rom. 3:23 (NKJV)*

In the beginning, when Elohim God chose to begin, the heavens and the earth were created (Gen. 1:1). At some point angelic beings were created.[17] At some further point, satan staged a rebellion against God and sorely lost.[18] No doubt due to satanic activity, the earth became void and nonproductive (Gen. 1:2). And at some point, which could have well been 'before the beginning', the mind of God conceived a family created in His own image. Genesis 1:3 records how He went about realizing what He had conceived in His heart.

The first thing God did was to prepare an environment for His future family. He spoke into existence a universe that was designed to respond to truth. He said: *Let there be light.*

There's an old adage that says 'truth is the light'. It might have arisen from the fact that light and truth are often coupled throughout the Bible. Psalm 43:3 says *'O send out thy light and thy truth: let them lead me; let them bring me unto thy holy hill, and to thy tabernacles.'* Jesus declared in John 8:12 *'I am the light of the world'* and again in John 14:6, *'I am the way the truth and the life'.*

It is significant that God sent out light first. Every created thing that followed would be immersed in a spiritual atmosphere of light. Often glory is spoken of as radiant, as emanating from its source. The glory of God saturated His words and so, as light jetted forth, His very nature permeated the void and pierced the darkness. Spiritual darkness didn't stand a chance.

God desired a sacred covenant and collaboration with those He would create in His own image. So once He had established the environment, He then made specific declarations over man. God created man in His own image and encoded man to have dominion in the earth, captured in the well-known passage Gen. 1:26:

*And [Elohim] God said, Let us make man in our image, after our likeness: and let them have dominion over the fish of the sea, and over the fowl of the air, and over the cattle, and over all the earth, and over every creeping thing that creepeth upon the earth. (KJV)*

The very image of God, both male and female, was imparted to the spirit of the man that He created (v. 27). However man was physically formed and manifested later, as recorded in Gen. 2:7:

*And the LORD God formed man of the dust of the ground, and breathed into his nostrils the breath of life; and man became a living soul. (KJV)*

Note that man's spirit was conceived first, and then his corporeal self (his body). There are at least two reasons for this order in the creation of man. For one, God always first deals with the spirit, that is, the heart of a person. While the world judges by the outer appearance, God searches the heart (1 Sam. 16:7). When we are born again, our spirits are recreated. We are a 'new creature' in Christ Jesus the instant that we are born again, but this refers to our hearts.

When we receive Christ, we become a new species. The old spirit that could only produce sin and death is discarded—we receive new spiritual DNA, *divine nature attribute*. The rest of our Christian journey concerns getting our soul (reasoning and emotions) and our flesh in line with the miraculous and perfect work that Jesus has done in our hearts.

(An aside: By the sheer mercies of God, my son turned out all right as a young adult. He's headed for graduate school in political science; he's fluent in Japanese and learning Chinese and Turkish. He has led several college mates to Christ. His parents are so grateful. But I wish that I had discerned his heart more and wrung my hands over his teen-age antics less. It was only when I began to understand my son's heart and stop reacting to his antics that various issues actually got resolved and his personality and outlook (realm of the soul) improved for the better. I'll listen to the hearts of my grandchildren.)

Secondly, God could have spoken the entire man into existence, spirit, soul and body, but He chose to be more involved in making us. Through the description in Gen. 2:7 God wants to convey to us an even more tender and intimate experience. There's no way to breathe into someone's face that is lying on the ground without stooping and cradling his head. It's almost frightening to write on the page of this chapter that, symbolically at least, *God stooped for us*.

*What is man that You are mindful of him?*

How can Someone so powerful—all-powerful, in fact—be so humble, be so gentle? There is so, *so much* to learn about the glory of God, the essence of Who our heavenly Father is!

After Adam became a living soul, Chapter 2 of Genesis records that the Lord provided Adam a beautiful garden—the garden of Eden, and an occupation, specifically, to name the animal kingdom and to cultivate the garden. Only one thing was now lacking. A man who possesses the spirit of God, communes with God, and has a good job is now qualified to have a wife (Gen. 2:22). Adam and Eve were a perfect match because God was the match-maker. He knows which two ribs go together, and when.

**The Tragic Fall from Glory**. Note Genesis 2:25 mentions that Adam and Eve were naked, but not ashamed. (There is much significance in this observation that we'll see later in context.) Adam and Eve had been commanded to enjoy all the fruits in their beautiful garden save one; they were not to eat of the tree of the knowledge of good and evil.

Some might wonder why God set things up this way. I believe that it's because God desired Adam and Eve to love Him by an act of conscious will. The only way such love could manifest is if Adam and his wife had a choice. If they didn't have a choice, then their existence was just a video game. God is certainly capable of choice, and thus His children, who were created in His image, are also capable of choice.

Unfortunately they chose wrongly. However, it was not without the assistance of shrewd deception. The serpent that had been possessed by satan slithered into the garden. We read in Genesis 3:1:

*Now the serpent was more subtle than any beast of the field which the LORD God had made. And he said unto the woman, Yea, hath God said, Ye shall not eat of every tree of the garden? (KJV)*

Notice that the serpent irreverently downgraded 'Lord God' to 'God'. The world doesn't mind you having a god as long as he's not the Lord. They don't mind you being religious as long as it possesses no power. They don't mind you giving respect to 'the man upstairs', but will resist the mention of Jesus. Why? Because Jesus is Lord, and the very mention of His Name torments demonic spirits. That's why in the secular world, there's toleration for the strangest of religious practices, but the name of Jesus is taboo.

The devil *thinks* he knows what he's doing. He's mistaken—he's going to lose anyway.

The enemy was able to sow seeds of doubt into Eve, and instead of casting down every thought that exalted itself against what she knew about God (2 Cor. 10:5), she bought into the lie the serpent had planted. God was dethroned in her heart, and satan had his in-road. Eve convinced her husband to rebel with her, and both of them ate of the forbidden fruit. Instantly, they realized that they were naked.

What do you mean, Adam and Eve realized that they were naked? They were naked in Chapter 2. How is it that they just now realized that they are naked in Chapter 3?

After Adam and Eve ate the fruit, for the first time, *they felt a breeze against their skin.* They felt cold, vulnerable, and exposed. Instinctively they sought to construct covering from leaves and vines. Why would they do this? **Because they had been accustomed to being covered.**

Covered with what? Why **God's glory**. Mammals have fur, reptiles have scales, and insects have exoskeletons. All of these creatures are covered with something. *We who were created in the image of God were meant to be covered with glory.* Psalm 8:3 says this about humankind:

*For You have made him a little lower than the angels[19], and You have crowned him with glory and honor. (NKJV)*

When Adam and Eve sinned, the glory that covered them immediately departed and they were acutely aware of it. Just that quickly, even as the morsel of fruit still traveled down their throats, the glory of God departed from humankind. Their spiritual DNA had been permanently perverted by sin. They had fallen from the glory of God.

Instinctively, Adam and Eve hid themselves from God. Sin had changed the relationship between God and His children. Instead of being drawn to the Lord, and eagerly anticipating His visit each evening, they no longer desired to see Him.

When God came to visit them in the cool of the day, of course He already knew what had happened, indeed, as pointed out in a previous chapter of this book, He *foreknew* what would happen. But He led Adam through a series of questions.

God asked Adam, where are you? (Now that you've made this decision to rebel against Me, where psychologically are you?) Adam's reply was that he was afraid, he was naked, so he hid himself.

Adam and Eve had learned something new, all right. Three foreign words, words never spoken before: fear, nakedness, and hiding.

I can only imagine how, for the rest of their lives, our poor original parents would long for the glory covering and those glorious days of fellowship with God that they had forfeited by sinning.

> Adam and Eve knew what it was like to be covered by
> God's glory and they sorely missed it.

One of the sure signs of a base culture is extreme immodesty, which tragically is the norm, literally the baseline in the present day. The pulse of our post-modern culture is so out of sync with God's heart and His holy standard that many people don't even realize that it's *shameful* to be indecently uncovered.

> In fact, *their glory is their shame.*[20]

I'm not talking about being ashamed of one's body—we are fearfully and wondrously made. To go too far in the other extreme is to assault the creative license of God that created us *in His image*. The human body is absolutely a physiological wonder and an aesthetic masterpiece. But there should be a pang for the loss of its original glorious covering, the Presence of God.

There is in fact a void imprinted in the core of each one of us that only the Lord can fill. There is a hunger that only God's grace can satisfy. No deed or vice can supply this hunger. There is a void in each of us that desperately needs the radiance of God's love. Truly the only life-force that can fuel us is the glory of God.

Well, how did it turn out for our original parents after their fall? Even though Adam and Eve egregiously failed the one test of loyalty that God placed before them, God did not abandon his failed first couple, or drop them right then and there. The consequences of sin were indeed grave and dire, but God had already conceived a master plan of redemption that He set in motion with the pronouncement that the seed of the woman would bruise the head of the serpent (Gen. 3:15). The seed of the woman would contain the source of our deliverance—and His Name would be Jesus.

# 5

# As Surely as I Live

*...As truly as I live, all the earth will be filled with the glory of the Lord. Num. 14:21 (KJV)*

*For as the waters fill the sea, the earth will be filled with an awareness of the glory of the Lord. Hab. 2:14 (NLT)*

God wants specific outcomes in the earth, but, inexplicably, He has bound Himself to us to obtain them. As example, He has determined to present to Himself a glorious Church, a Church that is a reflection of His glory (Eph. 5:27). Amazingly, this is a calculation that directly involves us!

God is certainly going to get what He wants, but He will never break His own rules to do so. In Genesis 1:26, God declared that man and woman should have dominion in the earth, and He's not going to renege on that declaration. For some reason 'that passeth understanding', God chose to yoke Himself to us through covenant relationship in order to achieve His ultimate purpose in the earth.

Tragically, those created in God's image, which had fallen from glory, grew comfortable in that fallen state and 'waxed worse and worse'.[21] Throughout the ages that God engaged with humankind all too often they were so rebellious over so long a stretch of time that they wearied and vexed Him.

*...But you have burdened Me with your sins; you have wearied Me with your iniquities Is. 43:24 (NKJV)*

*But they rebelled, and vexed his holy Spirit: therefore he was turned to be their enemy, and he fought against them. Is. 63:10 (KJV)*

And at times, it is sad to say, even God's own people have grieved Him. What grieves Him most is the sin of self-preservation.

Today there still exists many self-preserving believers. As long as these self-preservers are entertained by signs and wonders, bells and whistles, it's 'all good'; they're on board for Christ. As long as the proposition is popular, it's fantastic. But if it doesn't thrill them, or keep thrilling them, or if there is slightest hint of social disapproval or persecution, they bail out, they abandon the cause; they are nowhere to be found.

Recall the crowds in Jerusalem that hailed Jesus as the Messiah, spreading palms before His path one weekend—only to demand that He be crucified the very next weekend. Despite all the mighty acts of deliverance that God had performed for Israel, their loyalties were tossed with every wind and *shifted with every trend.*

Even as our Lord Jesus was being praised by the pressing crowds, He knew condemnation would follow shortly thereafter from the very same mouths. The Lord was deeply grieved, as one of the terrible consequences of His people's shallowness would be that they would never experience lasting peace.

*When he [Jesus] came closer and saw the city [Jerusalem], he began to grieve over it: "If you had only known today what could have brought you peace! But now it is hidden from your sight," Luke 19:41-42 (ISV)*

And lest we think that disappointing God was only the fault of people in the past, the text in Ephesians admonishes the Church today:

*And grieve not the holy Spirit of God, whereby ye are sealed unto the day of redemption. Eph. 4:30 (KJV)*

It is staggering to contemplate that our God of such almighty power and glory would love us with such intensity, *allowing us the license to grieve Him.* God forbid that we should ever callously take that license. Know this, if the Spirit of God is grieved, it doesn't bode well for whoever has caused Him grief. It is a fearful thing to rebel and continue to make wrong choices.

God is grieved that He cannot share His choicest treasures with that callous child. He is grieved because He knows that the devil, the enemy of all humankind, lies in the lurch ready to devour and to prevent yet another soul from achieving his or her divine destiny.

It is possible to be a child of God in covenant with God yet miss out on His best.

Alas, so it transpired in the account found in Numbers Chapters 13 and 14.[22] The Jewish people had suffered four hundred years of hard labor as slaves in Egypt. The Lord had used Moses to miraculously deliver the entire nation of Israel from Egypt. After two years of travel, approximately two million Israelites reached the border of Canaan, the land that had been promised to them. At the Lord's command, Moses appointed twelve spies to search out Canaan and to bring back a strategic report. The men took 40 days to complete their mission.

When the spies returned, they met with Moses and all the people. Sure enough, the land of Canaan flowed with milk and honey. The men displayed grape clusters so huge that they had to be hoisted on a staff, as well as plump figs and other delicious fruit.

But the spies also reported bad news. The various indigenous tribes, Hittites, Amorites, *etc.* were strong, dwelling in the mountains and along the coastlands. The walls of the Canaanite cities were well fortified. Worst of all, the dreaded Anak tribe (descendants of the giants) dwelt there. Compared to the Anak warriors, the majority of the spies said they felt like grasshoppers.

Upon hearing this, the people began to wail. However, two of the spies, Joshua and Caleb disagreed and tried to dissuade the people's alarm. These two men had not forgotten all the miracles that the Lord had done, not the least of which was delivering the entire nation of Israel from Egypt. Caleb, having perfect confidence in the Lord, quieted the people and said:

*...Let us go up at once and possess it, for we are well able to overcome the land. Num. 13:30 (KJV)*

Caleb truly had unwavering faith in God. Unfortunately, the people disregarded his correct report, choosing instead to believe the assessment of ten of the other spies. They began to wail even more. Though Moses their leader, Aaron the high priest, Caleb and Joshua rent their clothes appeasing the people to not blaspheme the Lord, it was to no avail. The people had already completely internalized the grasshopper imagery, *just like that.*

Mob dynamics took over as they next determined to kill Moses, Aaron, Joshua and Caleb by stoning them. Then they would appoint a new captain and return to Egypt. Their actions spoke loudly:

*Slavery in Egypt is better than God's promised land full of giants.*

Not an *ounce* of faith in the God of Abraham, Isaac and Jacob. No respect for the covenant He had made their forbears. No imagination or passion for what better could look like, what being a sovereign nation could feel like. So consumed with self-preservation were these Israelites that there was no concern for future generations—they were willing to consign their *own children* to live under the cruel lash of the whip. No desire to risk anything for...*everything*!

God, we don't care about what You have done for us up till now. We don't want Glory. *We want Convenience!*

# 6

# GLORY REPRESENTED

*Let your light so shine before men that they may see your good works
and glorify your Father which is in heaven.*
*Mt. 5:16 (KJV)*

We have learned that the glory of God is His very presence and essence, the holiness and the potency of God Himself. As we mature in Christ, pleasing Jesus and experiencing His strong presence becomes more precious and imperative than any other pursuit in life. As we walk in increasing obedience to the Lord, more of God's divine nature shines through us, overshadows and rules over our mortal selves. With increasing accuracy, we represent to the world what Glory is.

Just as the sun sustains the earth giving it warmth, the glory of God sustains the entire universe (including enabling the sun to shine). In fact, in heaven, the glory of God will replace the sun as the sole source of light and warmth (Rev. 21:23). The glory of God is resurrection power; it is the source and force of life (John 11:4). The Bible records that Christ was raised from the dead by the glory of the Father, and in like fashion His glory has raised those who have received Christ from spiritual death into the newness of life (Rom. 6:4).

*The Glory of God contains the potency of His presence.* Transitioning from glory to glory—that is, being glorified—is paramount to experiencing more of God's presence. So, what are the signs that the glorification process is taking place in our lives? What are the indicators that we are maturing, that we are giving God glory *by properly representing God's glory*?

- In the presence of God is fullness of joy (Ps. 16:11, 1 Peter 1:8, Jude 1: 24).

- In the presence of God is abundant goodness and mercy. (Ex. 33:18, 19, Ps. 23:6).

- The presence of God invites both confession *and* solution that *in tandem* vanquish and destroy the ancestral sins, fears, and prejudices that have held us captive with an unmerciful, ever tightening chokehold (Ps. 27:4-5; Is. 6:3-8).

- The glory of God is full of grace and truth. (John 1:14) Mark the believer who walks in mature grace that honors holiness and truth. Not only will she or he experience victory, but even people in the vicinity of that worshipper—relatives, co-workers, hecklers—will be delivered as well (Acts 16:25-26).

- God's Glory and victory are inseparable. The Christian who esteems and honors the glory of God will walk in victory that gives glory to God (I Chr. 29:11, Ps. 91:14).

- God desires His Glory to be a holy atmosphere, from which we draw His essence, in which we move and breathe, and have our being (Acts 17:28).

Acts 17:28 suggests that we should depend on Christ as we depend on air. Just as we don't have to constantly instruct our lungs 'inhale, exhale, inhale, exhale', being aware of God's presence in us and the 'tug' of His guidance should become our default state, as automatic as breathing.

So what happens in the absence of God's glory? The short answer would be just the opposite of what we have described above.

- Instead of fullness of joy in divine purpose, the jabbing pang of having settled, and poisonous envy towards those who chose not to compromise

- Instead of goodness and mercy, the downward spiral of all who continue to rebel against God

- Instead of holy confidence, numbing paranoia

- Instead of confession and resolution, confusion and uncertainty

- Instead of walking in truth, managing lies (a cellphone for each 'role')

- Instead of clarity and transparency, secrecy and duplicity

- Instead of glorious victory, shameful defeat

Whoever seeks to save his own life will lose it (Mt. 16:25); whoever seeks to forge his own glory, will find shame; whoever seeks to manage his own destiny will miss out on it.[24] That ship is never going to dock. A life steered by rebellion will be steeped in regret.

Any human endeavor that is not in resonance with the will of God will eventually be damped out. Oh, it may have an impressive run; the wickedness may last a long time by a human yardstick. But as surely as *Elohim* God lives, the person, philosophy, army or institution that would obstinately resist His Glory is already doomed to destruction. The very fabric of this earth, that *God* created, is *incapable* of indefinitely supporting sin.

*The earth was designed for **Light** to be!*

Actually this should not be surprising. The earth is the Lord's and the fullness thereof. Romans 8:29 says that the whole of creation is longing for the manifestation of the sons of God—when we become the glorious Church, the Church of Jesus Christ without spot or wrinkle.

When just the opposite occurs, when there's too much sin, when one too many ordinances has been trampled, when evil is called normal and truth is called intolerable, the land becomes cursed to such a degree that it evicts the source of the sin. Isaiah 24:5-6 says:

*⁵The earth also is defiled under the inhabitants thereof; because they have transgressed the laws, changed the ordinance, broken the everlasting covenant. ⁶Therefore hath the curse devoured the earth, and they that dwell therein are desolate: therefore the inhabitants of the earth are burned, and few men left. (KJV)*

Job 20:27 says of a wicked person's actions *"the heaven shall reveal his iniquity; and the earth shall rise up against him." (KJV)*

This brings to mind an incident widely reported in the news cycle wherein members of a reprehensible terrorist militia in Africa were driven from their place of hiding by the unlikely coalition of snakes and bees.[25]

Saints, don't stop praying. Never underestimate the authority of God's kingdom. Somebody prayed in that country and the bees and snakes got drafted for the Lord's work. Keep praying, saints!

If Earth reacts to sin by becoming uninhabitable, how will the Earth respond as the Lord—in all of His glory—approaches closer and closer?

One of the ways that the Earth will respond is by *trembling.* Psalm 96:9 declares: *Worship the Lord in the splendor of His holiness; tremble before Him, all the earth. (NIV)* Ps. 97:4-6 goes into more detail as to the riveting effects of God's Glory on Earth:

*⁴His lightnings enlightened the world: the earth saw, and trembled. ⁵The hills melted like wax at the presence of the LORD, at the presence of the Lord of the whole earth. ⁶The heavens declare his righteousness, and all the people see his glory. (KJV)*

Last and most importantly, the Lord Jesus indicated that earthquakes in diverse places would be amongst the signs of His glorious return to Earth.[26] As we approach the end of this present dispensation, we may expect an increase in the frequency of earthquakes as a consequence of Glory rising, that is, the glory of God reclaiming His earth.

So to summarize, how should God's glory be represented by us and how will Glory be revealed to us as the day of the Lord Jesus' arrival approaches? How will we recognize it? The list below is hardly exhaustive, and some of the indicators will be developed further in later chapters. But this list is a good start as a primer.

- *Joy and increased Kingdom authority among believers.* The saints who "do know their God" are growing in grace. They know the difference between His voice and the clamor of the world. These saints will recognize the signs of their soon coming King in the news cycle. They will rejoice. The saints that are in the know will be strong and do exploits (Dan.12:32).

- *Paranoia and crippling fear among unbelievers.* (Ecc. 12:3-5) In striking contrast, paranoia, fear, and volatility (anger; 'short fuse') will characterize all unbelievers *and* casual Christians who have rejected or sidestepped the Romans 8:30 glorification process which is the *epic purpose* of salvation and justification.

- *Foolish or detrimental ventures.* Isaiah 60:2 foretells that gross darkness will cover people who have not received Christ (have not been born again). Darkness stands for spiritual and mental dullness; plans and ideas devoid of godly wisdom. Gross darkness therefore connotes extreme ignorance of God's ordinances, which pretty much describes most of society today.

Sadly, droves of people, both of the powerful and 'pedestrian' variety, will make decisions or engage in activities that range from foolish to downright detrimental. Society's appetite for deception will worsen (2 Tim. 3:13). Meanwhile, the media will applaud such a decision right up to the point that its outcome turns horribly south.

- *Increase in earthquakes and tsunamis.* The earth will tremble. Among other geological events, tremors, earthquakes, and tsunamis (caused by underwater earthquakes[27]) will increase in frequency.

The Glory of the Lord is filling the earth, just as God promised to Himself. And as it grows, the earth and its inhabitants—the people that dwell therein—must be affected. So hopefully you and I reside in the joy category. Hopefully, we are delighting in the Lord, moving along in the glorification process, navigating persecution like big boys and girls, and enjoying increased authority in God's kingdom.

And when we see with our eyes, or read online, or hear of the other categories of events, we will not fear or fret, but realize that these are just the signs of the times. Those emotions, decisions, and outcomes are just the material and empirical consequence of Glory rising in a fallen world.

# 7

## GLORY REVOKED
### (THE TRAGEDY OF KING SAUL)

*Do not cast me from your presence; do not take your
Holy Spirit from me. Ps. 51:11 (ISV)*

The utter devastation that results from the absence of God's glory is tragically exemplified in the life of Saul. Saul was a king of Israel who chose self-ambition and pleasing people over treasuring the presence and glory of God. His ill-fated choice cost him his anointing, his mental health, his kingdom, his life and the lives of his three sons.[28]

Saul was anointed king of Israel by no less than the venerable prophet Samuel (1 Sam. 10:1). Initially Saul was open to the Spirit of God. The Bible records that on one occasion, the anointing of God fell so potently upon Saul that he prophesied with the prophets, astounding those who knew him.[29] This account shows that initially at least, Saul was allowing God to use him in a different capacity than that to which his neighbors and kinfolk were accustomed. In fact, God promised the newly anointed king that if he would serve Him and faithfully lead His people, then God would make of Saul a great nation.

It's not clear at what point Saul began to deviate from his initial zeal to please God. Perhaps because he was tall and naturally handsome, he had grown accustomed to people making over his good looks. But the king began to succumb to the pressure of pleasing people that is imposed upon all leaders throughout their entire tenure. Saul overstepped his authority on a number of occasions. But the last straw, the offense that cost him his anointing, is recounted in 1 Samuel Chapter 15.

The Lord sent the prophet Samuel to give King Saul explicit instructions. Because the Amalek tribe had refused to give Moses and the children of Israel safe passage through their territory en route to the Promised Land, Saul was commanded to fight Amalek and kill everything, even the king and the livestock.

So Israel fought in battle, overcame Amalek and executed *most* of what God had commanded. However, at the urging of Saul's advisors, they spared the life of Agag, the king of the Amalekites, as well as the best of the livestock. Later, when Samuel arrived on the scene, the prophet heard the bleating of animals. Moreover he saw that Agag was still alive. The verdict of the King of kings had been trumped by Saul's obsession for pleasing people at any cost.

Saul had disobeyed a direct order.[30]  He had rebelled against God. In any military, the commanding officer that disobeyed a direct order would be stripped of his rank and court-martialed. Tragically, Saul received a sentence far worse than that. 1 Samuel 15:23 records the prophet's sobering judgment:

*For rebellion is as the sin of witchcraft, and stubbornness is as iniquity and idolatry. Because thou hast rejected the word of the LORD, he hath also rejected thee from being king. (KJV)*

How does Saul respond to the prophet's words? Flippantly!

[24] *And Saul said unto Samuel, I have sinned: for I have transgressed the commandment of the LORD, and thy words: because I feared the people, and obeyed their voice.* [25] *Now therefore, I pray thee, pardon my sin, and turn again with me, that I may worship the LORD. 1 Samuel 15:24-25 (KJV)*

'Okay, I did it. The people pressured me to spare the cattle (and Agag is royalty, a king like myself, *after all*). Now do 'that thing' you do: pray, wave your arms, get that over with, so that I can do this worship ritual and get back to business as usual.'

Clearly, from the tenor of Saul's response, he had not yet processed the fact that he is no longer king as of…NOW! Saul had not yet processed that the anointing on him, *God's glory upon him had been revoked.* For that reason, the prophet Samuel is more emphatic the second time, saying in so many words, *This is for real, my brother.* He repeats the judgment:

[28] *…The LORD hath rent the kingdom of Israel from thee this day, and hath given it to a neighbour of thine, that is better than thou.* [29] *And also the Strength of Israel will not lie nor repent: for he is not a man, that he should repent. 1 Samuel 15:28-29 (KJV)*

But now, the reply of the deposed king is sacrilegious if not hinging upon blasphemy, as Saul indicts himself even more:

[30] *Then he [Saul] said, I have sinned: yet honour me now, I pray thee, before the elders of my people, and before Israel, and turn again with me, that I may worship the LORD thy God. 1 Samuel 15:30 (KJV)*

Translation: 'Yes, yes, sin. Yes. I can see that you're a little upset there. But please don't make a scene. I can live with God dishonoring me and taking away His anointing and all that. But I can't bear you dishonoring me in front of the people. *Not in front of the people.*

Once again I implore that you walk with me so it appears to the soldiers and the people that you're with me, that all is cozy, *as I worship the Lord YOUR — not mine — God.'*

This was a horrible response that laid naked and bare Saul's core values. Placing man's glory above God's glory led to his steady descent into paranoia, mental torment, envy, sociopathic willingness to murder indiscriminately[31] and a mass campaign to destroy his successor David (which utterly failed).

It has now been years since the Anointing—that precious covering of Glory—had departed from King Saul. His palace was stately but cold. A stifling and toxic air of treachery and confusion circulated through it. The guards who stood in stoic readiness could not arrest the evil spirit that had claimed Saul's mind.

Saul had fought God's will so long that he forgot what resting felt like. He had so descended into darkness that he could no longer hear from God. *His life was without form and void and darkness covered his reasoning.* His spirit gasped for God's presence but only darkness fed him. Saul was suffocating.

Ever since David had ducked the first javelin Saul threw with the intention of killing him, David saw how pitifully a king unravels without God's covering. David had witnessed firsthand Saul's decent into darkness; the depravity of Saul's conduct after the Glory covering left him. The fallen king's spiritual bankruptcy left an abhorrent impression upon David.

David deeply appreciated the presence of God's glory, of which the anointing is a particular expression. David knew that the anointing of God had enabled him to kill the lion and the bear to protect his flocks, as well as the giant Goliath in battle (1 Sam. 17:36-37). He understood how priceless it was and what a privilege it was to dwell in the presence of the Lord, to behold the beauty of the Lord, and to inquire in his temple (Ps. 27:4).

In fact, later on in David's journey, after he himself had greatly sinned by committing adultery and sabotaging the hapless husband, David repented and implored the Lord to not take the Holy Spirit from him. David's desperate and heartfelt prayer comprises the powerful verse of Psalm 51.

*Do not cast me from your presence; do not take your Holy Spirit from me. Ps. 51:11, ISV*

In contrast to the anointing of God resting heavily upon David,

Saul's joyless life had spiraled out of control. Once more the fierce Philistines had surrounded Israel with a menacing army, but there was no word for Saul from the Lord. The king—who once had commanded the slaughter of *eighty-five* members of one priestly family because one of them, Ahimelek, had innocently helped David—now had no priest to advise him.[32]

Desperation leads to foolish actions. Terrified by the huge array of Philistines, Saul stooped to consulting a medium to receive advice.[33] The omen that Saul received portended only more terror: Israel would fall to the Philistines; he and his three sons would be slain in battle. This tragedy befell them the very next day.

And so it was that a man who lived to please people died at their hands. But it was far more tragic than that: honoring people over God had demanded a heavy and cruel price of Saul's soul. To earn that crust of moldy bread, Saul had forfeited his

- authority – the right to rule
- spirituality – the grace to rule
- stability – the wisdom to rule
- destiny – the outcome of rule
- progeny – the transference of rule

Not only did Saul's dismissal of God's anointing cost him severely, sadly it also doomed his future generations: all of Saul's sons died in battle. Like a withering vine, the house of Saul deteriorated until eventually it was no more.[34]

O little children, I see the Glory Rising. I see the signs of the times. I see the paranoia in the world and the *apostate* church. I see the increasing boldness and beauty, authority and reach of the *true* Church. My eyes are older now, but my spiritual discernment is a *lot* sharper.

My eyes *do* see the coming of the Glory of the Lord!

So this is not the time to cling to the world. This is not the time to follow the crowd. This is not the time for self-glory campaigns. This is the *worst* time to lean to your own understanding. This is the time to trust in the Lord. This is the time to hold on *even tighter* to God's unchanging hand.

*The wise shall inherit glory: but shame shall be the promotion of fools.*
*Prov. 3:35 (KJV)*

# 8

# WE NEED HIS GLORY

*And he said, I beseech thee, shew me thy glory.*
*Ex. 33:18 (KJV)*

It is my prayer that the reader is just the opposite of King Saul—instead of trying to get along without God's Glory covering, she or he covets *more* of God's glorious presence. Spiritual hunger for God is key. The intensity of godly hunger that the Lord desires us to develop is captured in Moses' profound journey, both in his authenticity and in how transparently he sought the Lord.

Previously we confronted Moses' dynamics with the children of Israel after taking two years to reach the border of Canaan (when he commissioned the 12 spies). Now we look at what happened to Israel a little over three months into their exodus from Egypt.

Moses and the children of Israel had just experienced tremendous and astonishing victory over Pharaoh and the Egyptians. Nearly two million Israelites had crossed the Red Sea, and all of the Egyptian army drowned in that same Red Sea. Forty-five days into their exodus, about 160 miles southeast of Goshen[35], the Israelites pitched camp in the wilderness of Sinai not far from the base of Mount Sinai where Moses had first seen the burning bush, another manifestation of God's glory.

Shortly thereafter, the glory of God rested upon the mountain, and the Lord called Moses up into the mountain, as recorded in Exodus Chapter 24:

*[17]And to the eyes of the sons of Israel the appearance of the glory of the LORD was like a consuming fire on the mountaintop. [18]Moses entered*

*the midst of the cloud as he went up to the mountain; and Moses was on*
*the mountain forty days and forty nights.  Ex. 24:17-18 (NASB)*

There, on Mount Sinai, the Lord God gave Moses the Ten
Commandments on two tablets of stone and also additional
canon detailing how God's people should govern themselves.
For forty days and nights, Moses was supernaturally sustained
by the Presence of God. What a glorious communion that must
have been!

But as always, people are like sheep.[36] Those camped at the base
of Sinai grew tired of waiting for Moses to return. Though Israel
had waited to be delivered from Egypt for 400 years, they fretted
over 'forty long days' without any word from their leader. Nor
had they learned how to get a prayer through on their own. So the
children of Israel demanded that the acting leader, Aaron, who
was also the high priest, make a golden calf for them to worship
instead.

What about thanking the Lord God who had delivered them
from four centuries of bondage? What about the Red Sea miracle
that only occurred three months ago? How could the people so
quickly dismiss God, I AM that I AM—the Creator of heaven and
earth—who had *recently* brought the Hebrews out of Egypt with
such extraordinary display of power—for an inanimate, lifeless
golden object?

Truly the people's demand was rebellion and debauchery at the
highest level. In anger, God sent Moses down from the mountain,
judged the worst perpetrators on the spot, and sent a plague upon
the people.[37]

Can you imagine how demoralized Moses felt at this point?
He's eighty years old at the time. And after all his struggles, his
sacrifice, his service as a shepherd (after having been a prince) for
forty years—

After all the plagues that terrorized Egypt and broke the iron will of Pharaoh, after the epic victory at the Red Sea and the aggravation from leading nearly two million folk—not even 100 days into the journey, these people had already rebelled and turned to other gods. Moses was overwhelmed; he had nothing more to give.

Therefore, in Exodus 33, Moses is asking God for *assurance*. In verses 12-13 of that Chapter he says, "You have been telling me, 'Lead these people,' but you have not let me know whom you will send with me." He further says, in so many words, "Lord, You tell me I have found favor with you. Then please teach me Your ways so that I may continue to have favor with You. Remember this is *Your* project. These are *Your* people."

To every leader, doesn't *that* sound familiar!

Now the Lord graciously assures Moses, 'I will do all this for you and My presence will go with you'.

To borrow a phrase from one of my colleague, let's unpack verses 12-14. Notice that Moses first asks the Lord God to teach him *the ways* of the Lord. God responds by saying, 'My *Presence* will go with you'. Let's connect these dots.

An individual is unique because of the unique way he or she does things and responds to things. A person's ways define his or her personality. Extending this idea to Moses' conversation with the Lord, to take note of and respect the way God does things is to reverence God. And to reverence God is to invite His Presence.

The ways of God were not merely to be *memorized* (scriptures quoted). The ways of God were to be *executed* (life lived). We see that obedience to God's ways is a prerequisite to dwell in God's Presence and thereby experience His Glory.

In response to Moses' petition, Lord assured him that His presence would be with Moses. But Moses is desperate enough to persist (in so many words):

*You have given me charge and responsibility of over 2 million people. And I see in the first 100 days alone that this is too big for me to handle. Everything I've learned for the past 80 years has been debunked by this golden calf fiasco. If this thing is going to work, I NEED YOUR GLORY. SHOW ME YOUR GLORY.*

In yet other words, 'Not trying to be ungrateful or greedy, Sir, but':

- I need a LOT of Your Presence.
- I need Big Presence.
- I need Presence that *COVERS TERRITORY*.
- *I NEED YOUR GLORY!*

I have a question for you, especially for those called in areas of leadership: How many more trials and setbacks are you going to go through before you realize that you need His glory?

To walk in the good works that Christ has assigned to us (Eph. 2:10), we need His glory to shine on the inside *and* we need His glory to <u>confirm</u> on the outside. Those good works—works that you were ordained to walk in—will never be realized without God's glory involved!

The person that God's going to use to change this world for His glory will receive his or her heavenly assignment by Glory and will continue to seek God's presence in order to fully execute God's assignment. To perform the wonders of God, to change this world for Christ's glory, *you have to be a glory-addict.* Your fuel—your meat and your drink—has *got* to be the presence of God where the glory of God will always be found.

Moses was a glory-addict. He asked God, implored God urgently, 'Just *show* it to me already! ... Please.'

Next, an amazing event happens that reveals an eternal principle. God actually shows Moses—a mortal—His glory, as much as could be shown without killing Moses. In so many words, the Lord told Moses directly:

*No man can look at my face and live.* (Just as electricity always flows from high potential to low potential, Glory (high potential) will always 'electrocute' sin (low potential)). *Your flesh couldn't survive the pure, concentrated radiance.*

*But, here's what I'll do. I will hide you in the cleft of this rock. I will cover your face with my hand. Then as I pass by the rock, I will declare my goodness and my Name.*

Here, then, is the eternal principle: *God equates His goodness with His glory.* For most of us, God's glory brings to mind His 'external' attributes: power, majesty, sovereignty, radiance, etc. However, the first attribute that came out of God's mouth to describe His glory was His *goodness.* God is good! So we learn a profound truth:

God's character is the *source* of His glory.

Glory, power, majesty, sovereignty, and light itself derives from God's character, that He is GOOD.[38]

*Character* sources power. It's *never* the other way around.

If we tie this principle back to the glorification process, we see that transitioning from glory to glory requires us to *grow in the character of God.* Thus the glorification process in Romans 8:30 precisely intersects the *pruning* process in John Chapter 14, so as we grow in the character of God, we produce more fruit of the Spirit and good works. Jesus said: *Here's how you glorify my Father: bear much fruit* (John 15:8).

The fruit of the Spirit are listed in the beloved verse Galatians 5:23:

*Love, joy, peace, long-suffering, gentleness, goodness, faith, meekness and temperance.* These traits constitute the blessed and eternal character of our God, and they should increasingly describe each one of us who have received Christ.

(By the way, self-ambition, gossiping, and spreading division in the church does not make this list but they did make another list of the seven traits that are *detestable* to the Lord, found in Proverbs 6:16-19.)

What exactly does pruning entail? In gardening, pruning involves cutting away unnecessary outshoots from a plant or vine so that what remains grows more vibrantly. Analogously, our Heavenly Father sometimes allows difficult circumstances to remove distractions and wrong priorities from our lives. What I'm trying to convey is that pruning is seldom pleasant, but always necessary.

Every one of us was created by God to solve at least one problem. We have a huge assignment, and we need resources greater than ourselves to accomplish it. We might see wrongdoing around us, we are vexed by it, and we long for the power to right various wrongs.

Indeed, God desires for His Church to exercise supernatural power to solve problems; He sent the Holy Spirit to us for that express purpose. But the Lord will not allocate that power to a believer lacking character. We have witnessed the tragic end of personality after personality possessing a lot of power, talent, fame—but who was bankrupt in character.

So in Exodus 33, Moses had made precisely the right correlation: he sought to embody the character of God and be supported by the Glory of God as he led the people. Moses knew that it was the *only* way he would complete his glory-assignment, namely, get those two million people to the Promised Land.

The Biblical processes of glorification and pruning are complementary. Both address the same goal—building God's character in us—and both work for our good. We need the Glory to be able to endure the Father's pruning. We need the Father's pruning to be able to bear more Glory.

Remember: **the more Glory, the more territory**. So if we really seek to change our world in a manner that gives great glory to Jesus Christ, *we need the Glory!*

*Then Jesus said, "Did I not tell you that if you believe, you will see the glory of God?"*
*John 11:40 (NIV)*

# 9

# SALVATION AND GLORY

*…Alleluia; Salvation, and glory, and honor, and power,*
*unto the Lord our God:  Rev. 19:1 (KJV)*

Most of us don't hear a lot of preaching about Glory in church. But hopefully all of us hear a lot about grace and salvation. When it comes to presenting God's plan of salvation and inviting unbelievers to receive Christ, preaching the Cross of Christ and the grace of God is key. The grace of God—made possible by the Cross of Christ—*alone* saves us.

*For by grace you are saved through faith, and that not of yourselves, it is the gift of God.  Eph. 2:8 (KJV)*

*I have been crucified with Christ and I no longer live, but Christ lives in me. The life I now live in the body, I live by faith in the Son of God, who loved me and gave himself for me. Gal. 2:20 (NIV)*

'Grace' and 'Calvary' have to be in the conversation of salvation. My former pastor used to say that when he attended seminary, an older instructor would tell him: 'Son, whatever you preach, get to the Cross as fast as you can.'

And that is sound advice not only for preaching but teaching as well. Some may be familiar with the acronym for grace

**G**od's
**R**iches
**A**t
**C**hrist's
**E**xpense

that succinctly summarizes the *exceeding marvelous* outcome of the finished work of Christ.  How wondrous is the grace of God. How unfathomable is the love of Christ.  Forever we bless our God and thank Him for His amazing grace, His saving grace!  A beloved hymn declares:

> Grace, grace, God's grace,
> Grace that will pardon and cleanse within;
> Grace, grace, God's grace,
> Grace that is greater than all our sin![39]

Grace is transformative. As we allow the grace of God to continue its course, God's grace informs our personalities, motives, and behaviors. Receiving the grace of God through faith in Jesus Christ compels us to be grateful and motivates us to be more gracious towards others.

Without question, salvation is the most important of God's works; it is the triumphant expression of His eternal love. Salvation is so important that we are commanded by Jesus to actively execute its great commission: to go into the world, evangelize and win others to Christ (Mt. 28:19, Mk. 16:15-16).

It is safe to say that no matter the topic of a Christian book or teaching, it had better revolve around, or soon get around to Jesus Christ and salvation.  Otherwise, that book or teaching is not beneficial and needs to be tossed or deleted immediately.

With that said, this chapter aims to show from Scripture that when it comes to salvation, *God's Glory is involved from beginning to end*.  The entire proof could fill many pages; the more modest goal here is to present enough to convince.[40]

- **Restoring Glory is the goal of salvation.** First of all, the whole intent of salvation was to legally restore the glory of God to humankind without killing them. Colossians Chapter 1 exposes God's monumental plan of redemption that He had meticulously concealed:

*...The mystery which has been hidden from ages and from generations, but now has been revealed to His saints. To them God willed to make known what are the riches of the glory of this mystery among the Gentiles: which is Christ in you, the hope of glory. Col. 1:26-27 (KJV)*

Talk about controlling the message! The glory—brilliance—of the 'mystery' is that we who are born again now have Christ, the very source of Glory *inside of us*, ruling our recreated spirit man. *We are a new species.* We are coded with a new DNA.

*Divine Nature Algorithm.*

Now the daunting, but not impossible task that remains is to get our minds and bodies to agree with what Christ has masterfully accomplished in our spirit man.

- **Resurrection is an act of Glory**. Resurrection, an *essential* work in salvation's narrative, is an act of Glory.

    - Jesus equated raising Lazarus from the dead to seeing the Glory of God.

*When Jesus heard that [Lazarus was ill], he said, This sickness is not unto death, but for the glory of God, that the Son of God might be glorified thereby. John 11:4 (KJV)*

*Jesus said to her [Martha], "Did I not say to you that if you would believe you would see the glory of God?" John 11:40 (NKJV)*

Oh my friends, there is a glory of God to see in salvation!

    - The Glory of God raised Christ from the dead:

*Therefore we are buried with him by baptism into death: that like as Christ was raised up from the dead by the glory of the Father, even so we also should walk in newness of life. Romans 6:4 (KJV)*

- One day the glory of God will resurrect all from the dead. In particular, the Apostle Paul remarks of believers who have died:

*So also is the resurrection of the dead. It is sown in corruption; it is raised in incorruption: It is sown in dishonor; it is raised in glory: it is sown in weakness; it is raised in power: 1 Cor. 15:42-43 (KJV)*

- **Salvation reveals God's Glory**. Jesus, whose Name means *Salvation* walked in the glory He had received of His Father. Jesus' earthly ministry showed humankind what the glory of God looked like. Love or hate it, they were exposed to His graciousness and His truth.

*And the Word became flesh and dwelt among us, and we beheld His glory, the glory as of the only begotten of the Father, full of grace and truth. John 1:14 (KJV)*

- **Salvation imparts God's Glory**. Through salvation in Christ, Glory has been deposited in each of us.

*And the glory which You gave Me I have given them, that they may be one just as We are one. John 17:22 (KJV)*

> **only a mature Church leaning on Glory**
> **will ever become One.**

- **Salvation advances like Glory**. Like Glory, the agenda of salvation is *territorial*:

*Surely his salvation is near them that fear him; that glory may dwell in our land. Ps. 85:9 (NKJV)*

Salvation *indwelling* a person should progress to glory *dwelling* in a land.

- **Salvation enforces like Glory**. Deliverance from enemies *accompanied by gain in territory* is always an act of salvation, and therefore an act of Glory. Note the striking similarity between the rally of Moses just before God split the Red Sea:

*And Moses said unto the people: Do not be afraid, stand still, and see the salvation of the LORD, which he will accomplish for you today: for the Egyptians whom you see today, ye shall see again no more forever. Ex. 14:13 (NKJV)*

and that of a prophet addressing King Jehoshaphat and his people before battle:

*You will not need to fight in this battle. Position yourselves, stand still and see the salvation of the LORD, who is with you, O Judah and Jerusalem!' Do not fear or be dismayed; tomorrow go out against them, for the LORD is with you. 2 Chr. 20:17 (NKJV)*

In both cases, the enemies of Israel were devastated, and the children of Israel gained victory, freedom, spoil, treasure, or some important commodity that translated into ***a gain in territory***.

Enlarge our territory, Lord, as we glorify You![41]

- **Salvation is paired with Glory in praise.** Last but not least, salvation and glory are invoked together in joyful praise to God:

*In God is my salvation and my glory: the rock of my strength, and my refuge, is in God. Ps. 62:7 (KJV)*

*And after these things I heard a great voice of much people in heaven, saying, Alleluia; Salvation, and glory, and honor, and power, unto the Lord our God: Rev. 19:1 (KJV)*

From this brief exposition, we see that

- Glory conceived and supports salvation

- Glory fuels grace and
- grace enables us to give God great glory.

In fact, the global spreading of salvation by a vibrant Church fitly joined together is the very mechanism by which God will fulfill the promise He made to Himself in Numbers 14:21—that His Glory would fill the earth as the waters cover the sea. *Absolutely brilliant*. The wisdom of God is *stunning*.

But do we expect anything less from our great and awesome God?

# 10

# WHERE GLORY HEALS

*Then your salvation will come like the dawn, and your wounds will quickly heal. Your godliness will lead you forward, and the glory of the Lord will protect you from behind. Is. 58:12 (NLT)*

Somebody reading this book is experiencing deep emotional pain. Someone else is struggling to live a holy life, but keeps reverting to a terrible habit that may be properly called a *stronghold*, as it wields such a vice grip over his or her will. These statements are not based upon prophecy, but, rather, statistics. Every human being is a target for the devil and some of his fiery darts found their mark.

The devil is pathologically cruel, choosing to deeply wound many precious souls in childhood, either by hurtful words, or inappropriate intimacy imposed against their will; via abandonment/death of a parent or being spiritually broken by bullying and other abuses.

As children, we may not have known how to call on the Name of Jesus, or where to turn for help. However, all humans have a survival instinct: one's own mind tries to protect him or her from the raw pain by burying 'the Pain' so deeply into the subconscious that he or she felt safely estranged from it. But there it remains, like a spring-loaded booby trap, ready to trip us the rest of our lives whenever the enemy feels like pressing the self-destruct button.

Yet another huge way that the enemy ensnares people and holds them prisoner is through prejudice and erecting cultural barriers.

Children were carefully taught whom to hate, whom to fear, whom to despise and ignore. If the devil could keep all of us separated by tribalism, we would never unite and together forge solutions that unseated him.

Even after receiving Christ, the core damage that occurred in childhood had so permeated and fused into the psyche of so many of us, that we simply couldn't distinguish the script imposed by 'the Pain' or the 'tribalism' from our true selves.

The perverted perception was the only reality we knew.

Until Jesus came, enslaving people's emotions and thoughts was the trump card of the devil. Along with that leprosy called sin, poor self-esteem and prejudice were hostage territories that no positive thinking could wish away, no physical army could conquer, and no legislation could banish. After all, as a man thinks, so he is. *Whosoever owns the thoughts owns the man.*

The core of fallen man was chained to the father of lies. All efforts were vanity—whether noble accomplishment or nefarious treachery, religious ritual or secret sin—all were alike, all were dead works because *none* of them were motivated for, or by, the glory of God.

**But thanks be to God**, *Christ came to save us.* And thanks be to God, He stayed on that Cross until every destructive ordinance planned by satan against us—past, present, future—was *nullified*. And because of the thoroughness of the finished work of Calvary, Glory was authorized to cross boundaries and regain territory that had not been possible before. Jesus Christ gloriously triumphed over the devil and hell, and in that act of mighty redemption, Christ reclaimed spiritual and temporal territories that absolutely gutted satan's authority (Col. 2:14-15).

Truth and good news: The Glory of God can take over *wherever* He pleases, not only physically and materially in the earth, but spiritually and emotionally as well as in the past, present and future. Breadth, length, depth and height all belong to God.[42] Having said that, whenever God displays His Glory, His pure motive is to save people or to correct an injustice; it is never just for a flashy show of power.

We have dealt with Glory's mastery over both physical and spiritual death in the previous chapter. However, there are at least three other territories that Glory can infiltrate that no other agency can address or control:

> (1) deep-seated sin
> (2) areas of brokenness
> (3) prejudice and racism

Let us review each in turn:

**(1) Glory can surgically remove deep-seated sin**. In Isaiah 6:1-8, the prophet Isaiah experiences a tremendous vision of the Lord God sitting in great majesty. God's Throne-room was filled with smoke and the very pillars shuddered as angelic beings ministered to the King, loudly proclaiming: *Holy, holy, holy, is the Lord of hosts: the whole earth is full of his glory*.

There is something about the Glory of God that is so holy and exacting that sin *volunteers* to expose itself. Isaiah probably thought that he was an okay person, a pretty decent prophet. But in the presence of God's glory, Isaiah told on himself: *Woe is me, for I am a man of unclean lips and I dwell around similar people, so it's hard for me to escape the unclean lip thing*.

Isaiah's true self was finally able to articulate what Isaiah's pride had probably tried to suppress and deemphasize. (Kill the pride in us all, Lord!) You see,

> *when Glory rises, not only is the Glory of the Lord revealed,*
> *but so is everything else.*

In that atmosphere of Glory, God does not reprove Isaiah. By confessing, the prophet has already reproved himself! Instead, an angelic being places a hot coal directly on the prophet's lips that purges the iniquity—whatever was the source of his shortcoming. The 'potty mouth' is instantly solved.

*When Glory rises, confessed sin or shortcoming gets resolved.*

Note that it didn't matter when the sin was conceived, or how it was conceived, or how long it had held sway over Isaiah's life. It could have been a generational curse on Isaiah's family tree or just a bad habit he had picked up from the company he kept. It could have stemmed from a traumatic experience from his childhood. No matter. Once Isaiah confessed his sin, God was faithful and just to forgive him and to cleanse him from all unrighteousness (1 John 1:9).

And as if Isaiah's deliverance wasn't remarkable and generous enough, the Lord God next commissions Isaiah. He asks, *'Who will go and be my spokesperson? Who will talk for me?'* You see, Isaiah was called to be a prophet, but the stronghold of unclean lips would have crippled his effectiveness and also called into question his integrity as an agent for God. But now that Glory had evicted that stronghold, Isaiah was able to say, *Here I am, Lord, send me!*

*When Glory rises, pure and potent ministries are launched.*

Isaiah went on to become one of the most powerful, poised, and prolific among the prophets of the Bible. He predicted events concerning the Lord Jesus' life with such precision and clarity that he has been nicknamed *the eagle eye prophet*[43]. Isaiah's induction by Glory kept him on the straight path throughout his entire ministry. It's one thing to be called. It's quite another to consistently walk in integrity in one's calling.

Now fast forward to more recent times. The mothers of the church will tell you about how God would move in a prayer service so powerfully that if a drunkard stumbled into the sanctuary, he or she left sober and filled with the Holy Spirit—all the stench of alcohol erased. Thanks be to God for His power and glory!

Folks: Every sin in our lives can't take 30 years each to discover or conquer. Christ in you, the hope of Glory offers a much more efficient way. The more Glory, the more territory, and in many (not all) instances, the more Glory, the less time it takes to possess that territory.

**(2) Glory can heal brokenness from the past**. Glory can step backwards in time and undo the very source of the brokenness. In the gospel of Luke 13:10-17, we read of Jesus teaching in the synagogue on a certain Sabbath. As Jesus taught the congregation, He saw among them a woman who was bent over. Some translations say that she was bowed over. The Lord Jesus discerned that the woman had been in this condition for eighteen years and that her condition was due to an evil spirit. He also discerned that she had no power within herself to overcome the evil spirit and to stand straight.

Unfortunately, life has done that to many precious people in the world today. Even in the Church, even among the saints, we greet each other with practiced holy-speech, most of us stand straight; outwardly we look successful. But the sad truth is that some believers have been so battered and abused throughout life that mentally they are broken. They speak of victory in Jesus, but there's a gaping disconnect between their redeemed spirit and their broken soul.

Physically these precious people may stand tall, but in the spirit they have bowed to the oppression. Unless a power bigger than themselves advocates for them, they will never stand up in the spirit. These bowed over, *bowled over* believers will attend church—just as that dear woman in the Luke text attended synagogue, week after week for eighteen years, thirty years or more, say amen at the benediction—**and then go back home in**

**exactly the same bowed state that they came**.

But glory be to God, Luke records that *this* Sabbath morning, the bowed over woman received help from an Anointing that was bigger than her own. Jesus spoke to the infirmed woman and laid hands on her. Immediately she straightened up and gave glory to the God who had healed her by His Glory (vs.13)!

When the ruler of the synagogue and Jesus' adversaries protested, Jesus rebuked them. Glory had reached back to the covenant that God had made with Abraham and his descendants nearly two thousand years earlier.[44] Based upon that covenant, countered Jesus, the woman who was a daughter of Abraham ought to be delivered from the spirit of infirmity that had illegally oppressed her, Sabbath day or not.

And guess what: What the devil did to affront us was also absolutely illegal. And we don't have to be crippled by it another moment. As sons and daughters of Abraham, and even more so, as heirs of Christ,[45] we absolutely have the right to stand up tall, to walk in Kingdom authority, and to receive our God ordained blessings. Let us resolve to no longer walk this walk in Christ bowed to any pain or weaknesses of the past. Let the Glory of the Lord rise among us!

**(3) Glory alone can eradicate bigotry and cultural prejudice**. And finally, Glory will surely shut down the very hostile territory of bigotry. Moreover, the demise of bigotry will never be achieved by political will alone, honorable as such an endeavor might be: the alleviation of bigotry and prejudice *has* to be a work of Glory.

I feel compelled to spend a moment on this last topic of Glory tackling prejudice[46], for I believe that all things are possible with God.

In Acts Chapter 10, the apostle Peter has an unsettling dream in which he is invited to eat an array of various animals. As a Jew, the apostle had been taught at a very young age that certain animals were unclean. These were the very animals he saw in his dream. So while in dream state, Peter protests to the Lord, 'Not so, Lord: for I have never eaten that which is common or unclean'.

*Prejudice (of any sort) is taught from childhood.*

God told Peter 'don't call unclean what I have cleaned up!' Three times this exchange occurred—removing prejudice may take several passes. When Peter awoke, he knew that he should preach the Gospel to the Roman centurion Cornelius and his household, even though they were Gentiles. The Gospel of Jesus Christ was for *outsiders* as well!

Note that Peter was enlightened and freed from his cultural bias *while in a deep dream*. The Holy Spirit addressed Peter's core being. Peter's core being got fixed, and now he was free to obey Jesus and preach the Gospel to *whosoever will*.

Entrenched prejudice rules from the subconscious of a person. A person trained to be prejudiced is *incapable* of regarding 'the other kind of folk' as equal. And even a 'guilt-ridden bigot' is still a bigot. They will throw money at a societal problem, but refuse to invest in the *conversations* and *physical presence* that are necessary to forge reconciliation and establish relationship. Liberalism is no match for tribalism. Only a Glory atmosphere has the authority and reach to snatch someone who is entrapped in tribalism, racism and the like. *This kind of devil gets ejected only this way*.

The Glory is coming. Glory is Rising. The Gospel of Jesus Christ must be preached everywhere. Glory has got to reach everyone. Disciples of Christ have to be raised up on every landmass: continent, island, and archipelago. That's why I know that before Christ returns, the end of cultural and racial prejudice—in the Church at least—is inevitable.

When Jesus does come back for His glorious Church, in *that* Church, it's going to be on earth like it is in heaven. Don't relegate to heaven the virtues that God meant to be achieved on earth: whoever would mature in Christ is not only going to love all people *then*, he or she must be willing to learn how to love more people *now*.

In conclusion: if your heart is broken, like the bowed over woman—if you struggle with a persistent sin, as did Isaiah, or, if like the apostle Peter, you disregard certain types of people, please know that Glory can heal our subconscious. Deeper can reach deep (Is. 42:7, Heb. 7:25). Glory can purge the conscience from dead works including the Pain, the Shame, and the Hatred (Heb. 9:14). Glory can step back into the past and deliver the child from that debacle so that, going forward, he or she grows to be a beautiful, powerful, and fearless vessel for God's glory.

This is a good time to say 'Thank You, Jesus!'

# 11

## GLORY TO GLORY: HOW GLORY RISES

*But we all, with open face beholding as in a glass the glory of the Lord, are changed into the same image from glory to glory, even as by the Spirit of the Lord. 2 Cor. 3:18 (KJV)*

When I was (much) younger, my family would take road trips. Being raised in mid-Michigan, landscape was mostly flat. My hometown was located in a broad valley, however you'd never know it for looking. But seventy miles north of town, the interstate would narrow and curve, the pines loomed taller and there were more hills. It was a whole new world, where adventure might erupt just beyond the pine tree line. I used to love to look at the scenic woods, soak in their ancient and pristine beauty, and feel the rush in my stomach as the car winded up, then down, then up again the hills.

It turns out that maturing in Christ proceeds in much the same way. Our Christian journey is seldom, if ever, a linear path; instead, there are curves in the road, detours, side excursions, ecstatic high points and dreary, perhaps devastating low points. The good news is that God foresaw everything that would happen to us, before the worlds were even created. For the believer who pursues God's purpose, all those collective experiences are engineered by Christ to *precisely accomplish* his or her God-sanctioned destiny.[47][48]

So let's think for a moment about *how Glory rises* in that Christian journey. We had previously established a connection between the glory to glory process in 2 Corinthians 3:18 and the glorification process in Romans 8:30:

*Moreover whom he did predestinate, them he also called: and whom he called, them he also justified: and whom he justified, them he also glorified. (KJV)*

In Romans we see a sequence of progression designed for the benefit of the child of God with its final stage being the act of glorifying or glorification. The sequence is:

### predestined called justified glorified

Some may not be as familiar with justification, so I'll briefly describe it. Justification entails being born again, becoming a new creation in Christ Jesus (our spirit man being recreated). It's *how* we are born again, the miraculous process that removes the stony heart and gives us a new heart that is receptive to God's heart (Ez. 36:26).

But justification also contains a bigger *legal* significance. It's also *why* we can be born again. Most importantly, Jesus' *propitiatory* or substitutionary work—bearing our sins and dying in our place—was entirely legal; it was *just* and *justifiable*.

Jesus' sacrifice on our behalf didn't violate God's decree that humankind would determine the course of the earth (Gen. 1:26-28), because He did not come to earth as Creator God. He was born like other human beings. Both Jesus' birth in a manger and death on the Cross were essential on legal grounds so that God would be *just and the justifier of whoever has faith in Jesus* (Rom. 3:26).

So back to the process of Romans 8:30:

### predestined called justified glorified

Of these four stages, three stages are either already completed or instantly transacted for the believer:

- We had *nothing* to do with God's predestination decisions. We could not elect ourselves. (We didn't even exist yet, except in the heart of God).

- We had *nothing* to do with the call. God did the calling. And once we said *yes* to His call of salvation and received Christ

- We had *nothing* to do with work of justification. All the hard work required for justification to be a free gift had been remitted by Christ on the Cross. When we receive Christ, we are instantly born again; we are instantly a new creation.

However, we _do_ determine how much of the *glorification* gets accomplished in us while on earth. Keep in mind that glorification is the goal of salvation; it is the climax of God's plan. And you and I determine how far into this last stage we progress on earth.

Now, glorification had been previously defined as the supernatural, *uninterrupted,* continual renewal of our minds. In Romans 12:2, the apostle Paul beseeches us to continue to renew our minds, to continue to spiritually improve. How might we give God more glory today? Then let's do *that!*

Glorification is the God directed journey from glory to more glory. It was the way God would keep that promise to Himself to fill the earth with the Glory of the Lord: by training His Church to adopt His character so that they could handle His Glory in increasing amount!

Long before God informed the deceitful serpent in the garden of Eden that He would destroy the devil's works, He already knew just how He was going to reinstitute goodness in His earth. God had already convened with the Lamb who would be slain on Calvary's Cross before the foundation of the world. He had already mapped out instituting glorification through the finished work of Christ.

When God served that sly snake in the garden of Eden, *glorification was already a done deal.*

Glorification is the end purpose of the divine plan of salvation. It's *why* you were predestined. It's *why* you were called. It's *why* you were justified (redeemed). It's the climax of every blessing and stage that God has laid out for us.

But Glory has the larger agenda of *enforcing mercy* in mind. There are problems you were created to solve, and people right now who are sighing or dying until you step up to the plate and solve them. But dear one, you will need the same thing Moses needed, **Glory**! To fulfill your *God sanctioned* destiny, you will need Anointing that's far bigger than yourself and that covers far more territory than a life lived for only convenience could ever authorize.

Submitting to glorification is our sacred duty.

So now we are on board for glorification. We truly desire to fulfill our God sanctioned destinies. But what does the process look like?

2 Corinthians 3:18 says that as we look upon the glory of God, we are changed from glory to glory. This beholding actually means to gaze, to fix one's eyes upon, to focus upon. The aim of the focus is to concentrate and stay with it until we get a concept, a picture. So we are to focus on the glory of God. Great, so how do we do that?

John 1:14 indicates that the Word of God is the revealer of God's glory: *And the Word became flesh and dwelt among us, and we beheld His glory... (KJV)*

We get a picture of Who God is by noting the things that Jesus did and the words that He taught. People already knew that God was powerful and sovereign, at least at the head knowledge level. All polytheistic religions ascribed those traits to their leading gods.

So Jesus came to show people that God is good, God is merciful, God is faithful and kind. (*And* can command the wind and the waves *and* can raise the dead whenever He likes). As has been pointed out, God's character is the source of His Glory, so to learn of God's holy character is to 'see the Glory of God'.

At this point a lot of sincere believers think: Great! I get it. Let's study our Bibles, pray, go to church, do right, do our best to avoid evil, and the glory to glory process will proceed as:

That was certainly my view as a young Christian. But the glory-to-glory process is actually more like a drive through upper Michigan—better yet, out West:

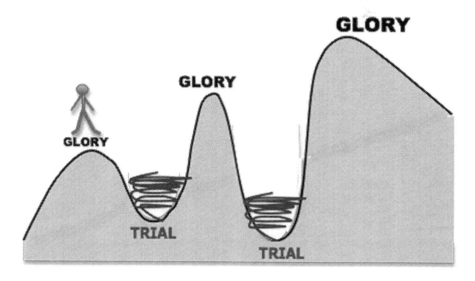

There are going to be *trials* between the triumphs, dark days and weary nights before the morning's bright dawn. As one pastor put it: new levels, new devils. Moreover, the diagram above suggests that the next trial is not necessarily easier, indeed it is usually deeper, but once we surmount it we are qualified to bear even more of God's glory for His purposes.

So, while the downside of attaining new levels is indeed new devils, the upside is that you're meeting them with more Glory and gaining more territory. When we think about all that the Lord has done, and where He has brought us from, we conclude: If He delivered the last time, He'll do it again!

In the next chapter let's think about the reasons for the up and down sequence in our God sanctioned 'glory to glory' journey. There are many more benefits to this pacing than you might think—and I pray you'll be convinced as to what an honor and privilege it is God has invited you to experience firsthand His Glory rising.

# 12

## LEADERS NEED UP AND DOWN

*...Who is like you, God? ²⁰Though you have made me see troubles, many and bitter, you will restore my life again; from the depths of the earth you will again bring me up. ²¹You will increase my honor and comfort me once more. Ps. 71:19-21 (NIV)*

*⁷ He lifts the poor person from the dust, raising the needy from the trash pile ⁸ and giving him a seat among nobles —with the nobles of his people. Ps. 113:7,8 (ISV)*

To fully appreciate the 'up and down' pattern of God's glorifying process, you have to understand that every one of us are called to lead in some capacity. Of course, not all of us are called to pastor, or to be a CEO, but all of us are called to be salt and light. If you are a parent or have charge over children, you are by default in a position to greatly influence the next generation. So it turns out that the Biblical vetting of all believers, whether leader or follower, is very similar in its rigor.

There are at least four reasons that God allows the ups and the downs (but always ending on an "up") in the glorification process: (1) It was Jesus' pattern on earth (2) it teaches humility (3) it develops empathy, and most times (4) the Glory is revealed in the valley. So let's look at each quality in turn.

**(1) Jesus' pattern**—The most compelling reason we may expect ups and downs in the glorification process is because the Lord Jesus, whose pattern of life we are to model, lived out His ministry this way. Jesus Himself reminded us, *the servant is not above the Master.* Jesus pioneered the Way—the only way—to experience more of God's glory here on earth. He is the One who first went through ups and downs for us.

*The one who went down is the same one who went up above all the heavens so that all things would be fulfilled. Eph. 4:10 (ISV)[49]*

*But he stripped himself and took the form of a servant and was in the form of the children of men, and was found in fashion as a man. Php. 2:7 (Aramaic)*

The first 'down' Christ experienced on our behalf was to strip Himself—some Bible translations say *to empty* Himself of His divine abilities, including the level of Glory to which He was accustomed. The ultimate low point was Christ becoming sin for us and His death on the Cross.

But a **monumental high point** was when Christ was raised from the dead by the Glory of the Father[50], making it possible for whosoever that would believe Him to be freed from sin and to obtain everlasting life. Glory, hallelujah!

**(2) Humility**—I'm going to spend a moment on this one, because it's a big one. Many want the benefits of the Glory cloud without paying the price to dwell there. The reason boils down to pride, which you could say is essentially self-glorification. Pride says 'I am such and such without God' or 'I can handle such and such without God'. Pride has "I" in the middle. God has no tolerance for human pride.

The curse of pride is pervasive in the fallen nature of humankind[51]. Let us not be fooled—we *need* some downs in life, else uninterrupted promotion after promotion and continual praise lavished upon our efforts would conceive pride. Consider poor Kanyé, the poster child for all mega-celebrities that the entertainment industry "selects". But we need not single out celebrities; no human being is exempt from the seduction of pride.

Unfortunately, many in the Church attempt to live their lives by the flawed model 'all blessings, no trials'. This superficial model of Christianity can sell books and fill stadiums but it can never secure that coveted place of God's rich presence or the authority to enforce good that *only* Glory provides.

Struggles and setbacks often serve as the remedy for pride. I did not say to pray for struggles—don't worry, they are coming or have already arrived! Oftentimes the struggle forces us to depend on the God that we often *quote* we depend on, as well as soften the rough edges in our personalities.

David saw the benefit gained from his times of struggle. He wrote in the Psalms:

*My suffering was good for me, for it taught me to pay attention to your decrees. Ps. 119:71 (NLT)*

As another example, the Apostle Paul was caught up to the third heaven—(can you imagine having the revelation of, say, the book of Romans disclosed to you for the *first time ever*?) However, Paul was brought right back down by a meddlesome thorn in the flesh (2 Cor. 12:9).

*And lest I should be exalted above measure through the abundance of the revelations, there was given to me a thorn in the flesh, the messenger of Satan to buffet me, lest I should be exalted above measure. 2 Cor. 12:7 (KJV)*

God did not want Paul to be ensnared by pride. So when the apostle sought—three times in fact—to have the thorn removed, God lovingly refused, because He knew what would spiritually stabilize his son Paul:

*My grace is sufficient for you. You need to be always reminded that you're the junior partner in this Glory collaboration so that at the end of your days on earth you receive ALL of the reward I intend to give you in heaven.*

The purpose of 'glory to glory' ups-and-downs is to develop the precious fruit of humility (and longsuffering) in our lives. God wants to establish in us a most unusual and unlikely alliance—a holy collaboration that defeats the enemy's devices every time: *great power steered by even greater humility.*

We have only to look at the life of Jesus to see the purest expression of humility. Though the fullness of the Godhead dwelt in Jesus[52], for our sakes, He endured hardships and inconveniences, even prior to His death on Calvary's Cross. It took humility just to go through human birth and live on earth with less Glory than that to which He was accustomed.

Jesus was despised, rejected, ignored and underappreciated. He was subjected to hunger, thirst, tiredness and weather. Yet Jesus humbled Himself even more to bear our sins and to die on the Cross. But, oh, oh, oh, what almighty consequence arose from that noblest humility! Philippians records:

[9] *Wherefore God has highly exalted Him and given Him a name above every name* [10] *that at the name of Jesus every knee should bow, of things in heaven, and things in earth, and things under the earth;*[11] *And that every tongue should confess that Jesus Christ is Lord, to the glory of God the Father. Php. 2:9-11 (KJV)*

Hallelujah Jesus is Lord!

Hallelujah for the downs, then ups.  That was our Lord's pattern that saved us. That is Glory's way to prepare us for our glory-assignment here on earth and for heaven afterwards.

*That is how Glory rises.*

**(3) Empathy (and Bridge Building).** (We've got to spend a moment on this attribute as well). A third reason for the ups and downs in the 'glory to glory' process is to increase our *empathy*, and thus expand our capacity to reach people. *There is no Glory-assignment* *from God that doesn't involve at some point breaking through a culture barrier and building a cultural bridge.*

Empathy is the ability to understand and share the feelings of others. Spiritually, empathy enables us to be compassionate. Compassion was the motivation of the greatest miracles that Jesus performed, including the resurrection of Lazarus and God so loving us.

Empathy is indispensable for Glory to rise in these last days. Jesus was touched with the feelings of our infirmities (Heb. 4:15), and if we desire to reach this world effectively for Christ, we must preach the Gospel *and* be genuinely touched by the sufferings of our brothers and sisters.

Lacking empathy, people possessing the ability to solve a problem have no inclination to do so, because *they simply don't care.* That is why racism and other forms of prejudice are satanic in origin: they build walls of callousness and mistrust between neighbors, cultures and communities. A good church may be in need, but other churches that could help that fellowship choose not to do so. One community suffers and another with resources or, more importantly, *prayer resource* simply doesn't care.

Prejudice is the enemy of empathy. Prejudice poisons compassion.

But our Lord was full of compassion. Jesus came to break down the middle wall of partition between us (Eph. 2:14) and has given us the ministry of reconciliation (2 Cor. 5:20). God desires His house to be a house of prayer for all people (Is. 56:7) and promises that He will fill His house with Glory (Hag. 2:7) And one of the major ways the Lord will accomplish this—filling His house with Glory—is by breaking down cultural and other prejudicial barriers, so that all sorts of people may freely receive Christ Jesus.

Any room full of saved folk with Christ the hope of Glory indwelling them and who are *wiling to work together* contains more power than the sun. But how does one unite people from different social status, racial groups, intellectual scope, and nationalities together for Jesus' purposes? How does one overcome the deeply entrenched prejudices that obstruct unity?

You see, prejudice is a daunting stronghold because it was presented as *the earliest of truth* to a child. It was poured into the concrete foundation of all she knows to be real. Prejudice reigns with an iron will on the throne of the confiscated heart; it occupies a high *wicked* place that no human logic can placate. At best, law might suppress it, but can never displace it.

> With man it is impossible to eradicate prejudice.
> But not with God!

In fact, only Glory can reach *and breach* the spiritual territory where prejudice reigns. Only Glory, performing deep and primordial spiritual surgery, can uproot this kind of perversity.[53]

To this end, by His unsearchable wisdom, God employs the same 'glory to glory' up and down sequence to develop empathy, especially in His leaders. For if the leader is wise and kind, those qualities will trickle down to his followers, just as the holy anointing oil poured upon Aaron's head and beard trickled down and saturated his robes (Ps. 133:2).

An extraordinary leader can reach out to people beyond his or her own race, culture, intellect, or nationality. A person in charge who can only relate to his own kind may be a *plantation foreman* or a *bully* but not a leader by God's standard.

As we strive for godly excellence in our Christian journey, we can be inspired by the extreme up-downing in social status experienced by four persons in the Bible. They went from poor to power or from rich to poor to rich again. All of their journeys took them to different lands where they had to learn a new culture and language. Their 'zig-zag' journey, directed by the Holy Spirit, caused them to become extraordinary leaders.[54] [55]

- **Moses**. This venerable leader was born to Hebrew slaves, raised in Pharaoh's palace as a prince of Egypt, but disgraced as a fugitive (criminal). Moses fled Egypt, then toiled 40 years in Midian as a shepherd. Once his training was completed, he was elevated to leader of over two million people. God used Moses to free all the Hebrews from Egyptian slavery and led them to the very border of their Promised Land.

  Note that though being a prince in Pharaoh's court was no doubt posh, Moses' influence in that capacity was not sufficient to free two million Jews from bondage. Simply being a prince didn't cover enough territory.

- **Joseph**, a handsome young man worth the equivalent of a billionaire by today's market, was sold into slavery, and then further demoted to prisoner. Once his training in administration was completed (started in Potiphar's house), Joseph was promoted to extraordinarily high rank in Egypt, second only to Pharaoh. His skillful and just disbursement of food saved Egypt and many other people in the region—his own family included—from starvation.

  Joseph's father Jacob was very wealthy, but Dad's wealth could not have saved the family from a seven year-famine. Being a billionaire alone didn't cover enough territory.

- **David** was raised by a God-fearing family, exposed to the protocol of the king's court then, due to King Saul's envy, labeled an enemy of the state. At one point, David had to hide in the cave Adullam with four hundred scofflaws—

quite a switch from his 'church boy' upbringing—he also had to spend a few years living in Philistia (an enemy's country). But then, once his training was completed, David was elevated to be king for 40 years over both Israel and Judah. Being raised in a nice family was wonderful, but that experience alone could not earn the territory God created David to possess: to serve as worshipper, warrior, and king.

- **Paul** is the most renowned of the apostles, having been inspired by the Holy Spirit to pen nearly half of the twenty-four books of the New Testament. After his conversion to the Way, Paul spent three years in Damascus receiving insight from Christ concerning His Church. Talk about being transcultural: you have a Jew and Roman citizen learning about Christianity in an Arabic country.[56]

  Additionally, Paul was already multilingual so he was wondrously prepared for global evangelism.[57] You can read about what Paul thought of his natural credentials compared to gaining Christ in Philippians 3:8.

In all of the cases just cited,

*MORE GLORY* meant MORE *TERRITORY.*

Every leader-in-training was exposed to what it was like to be poor (or a slave), and to be rich (or in the king's court), to be in good social grace, and to be a fugitive (or criminalized). These apprentices automatically developed empathy as they took on these various roles from extreme stations of life. And the outcome of these experiences? Such a leader could lead *everybody*.

So, before that next complaint about that relocation, or assignment to work with a different group of people on the other side of the building or on the other side of town, think again. Might it be an opportunity for God to expand your spiritual reach by increasing your empathy through the new situation?

God desires us to break down barriers and build up spiritual reconciliation. How will we ever 'go into all the world' if we won't even venture into the next neighborhood two streets away? So, Christ builds barrier-breaking roles into our 'glory to glory' journey.

The obedient believer will take courage and embrace the opportunities. And no, it won't be easy because it requires us to face and to assess ourselves. Those erroneous values taught from childhood must be deconstructed, and God's holy values take their place.

But the reward of preaching Christ in a more effective way and to a larger marketplace will more than make up for the discomfort of the training ground. The reward of rebuilding waste places[58] one family member, one neighbor, one neighborhood at a time will be so radiant and beneficial that all will give glory to God.

**(4) Glory is revealed in the Valley.** And finally, a benefit of the up-and-down pattern in the 'glory to glory' path is that the most precious jewels of truth and power are usually discovered while we're in the valley. The need to develop humility and empathy is precisely so God can entrust you and me with more revelation of His plan; so we can see a little more of it. The transference of revelation to us is precisely Glory rising in us; God's glory being revealed.

Jesus told us to consider the lilies, and so we shall: the Regal lily *(lilium regale)* may be found everywhere today, but nearly a century ago, this fragrant flower's only natural habitat was a 30-mile stretch of rocky cliffs in a narrow valley in the Hengduan Mountains in China.[59] There is a spiritual analogy:

> Some treasures of beauty will only be gathered
> or experienced in the valley.

In the Bible, the lily sometimes represents a type for Jesus Christ[60] or for revelation knowledge[61]. There are some truths and insights that can only be revealed to us in the valley, at midnight, in that moment just before the dawn. Over a century, ago the renowned clergyman Charles H. Spurgeon agreed, commenting in regards to hardships:

*I am certain that I never did grow in grace one half so much anywhere as I have upon the bed of pain. It ought not to be so. Our joyous mercies ought to be great fertilizers to our spirit; but not infrequently our griefs are more salutary than our joys. The pruning knife is best for some of us.*[62]

It is indeed unfortunate that the psyche of fallen man had been so distorted by sin that it usually takes suffering and pain to jumpstart a sincere, *unbiased* search for God. By unbiased is meant: one seeks the Lord with an open heart, without any preset notion of what to expect next.

When relentless persecution and pressure has so frustrated us; once it has worn us out and has brought us to the end of ourselves; at that very intersection, a Glory opportunity has been extended to us; an overwhelming victory is within our grasp, for *at the end of ourselves is the beginning of divine breakthrough.*[63]

The Apostle Paul elegantly said it this way: *And He (God) said to me, "My grace is sufficient for you, for My strength is made perfect in weakness." Therefore most gladly I will rather boast in my infirmities, that the power of Christ may rest upon me. 2 Cor. 2:9 (NKJV)*

The moment that we throw in the towel *for real* is the moment God takes over. He is *serious* about getting all the glory. God will sit on His throne and watch the devil wear you out until you're ready to sit at His feet and watch Him wear the devil out.

Whoops! Looks like I switched from talking about Glory to talking about how to get through a trial. Actually, no, because, the whole point of a trial is to wear down a little more of our dependence upon ourselves, so that more Glory can now shine through, whip more devils, and accomplish more Kingdom work through us.

So to summarize, godly leaders benefit greatly from the 'glory to glory' up and down model. In fact, all of us need ups and downs built into our journey because:

- It is the *model* that our Lord and Savior Jesus Christ pioneered for us.

- It develops *humility* so that we can safely handle increased power and authority required to carry out a larger assignment.

- It expands our *empathy* so that we lovingly reach out to others different from us and are genuinely touched with their pain.

- Some *divine revelations* (including strategies to crush satanic forces and to gain more territory for God's Kingdom) will only be found in the valley.

# 13

## GLORY GOING GLOBAL

*And the glory of the Lord will be revealed and all flesh will see it together for the mouth of the Lord has spoken it. Is. 40:5 (NIV)*

So far we have talked mostly about how the Glory of God impacts and transforms the child of God; how an increase in Glory increases his or her ability to live right and authority to enforce mercy. In other words, up to this point, we've thought mostly about how the Glory of God profoundly affects an individual.

But as the end of this present dispensation rapidly draws to a close—as that temporary construct called time gives way to eternity—there will be effects of Glory that the whole world will see, not just believers in Jesus. In fact some of the disparaging turmoil that headlines the news cycle is precisely due to Glory rising.

When one thinks about it, it's not really surprising that some Glory events will affect everyone. God made a powerful promise to Himself to cover the earth with glory as the waters cover the sea. Glory has been increasing ever since, as previous chapters have attempted to substantiate. Once God's glory reaches a critical concentration in the earth—whatever that number is— every square inch of the earth is going to respond dramatically to the presence of His glory!

One day I was driving home during a dramatic electrical storm. This storm vented with fury. The night was pitch black and raindrops were slamming into my windshield. The wipers 'scrambled' to remove the watery sheath, but it was still hard to see. Due to visibility, traffic had been reduced to a crawl.

Suddenly there was the brilliant flash of a horizontal lightning bolt[64] that arced from east to west. For a moment, that lightning bolt had electrified the entire horizontal view. Anybody who lived within 50 miles probably saw that lightning. The thought came to me: God's Glory will be like that. Just as everyone in the region would have seen the lightning bolt that I had just seen, one day, when the Glory of the Lord is revealed, all flesh will see it together.

*For as lightning that comes from the east is visible even in the west, so will be the coming of the Son of Man. Mt. 24:27 (NIV)*

Those scorners out there who jeer for God to prove Himself—be careful what you ask for. God is going to prove Himself, all right. There's going to come a glorious moment, when time is no more, that *every* knee will bow and *every* tongue will confess that Jesus is Lord (Php. 2:10, Rom. 14:11, Is. 45:23).

But even before that definitive moment of unfurled and uncensored truth, God is already revealing His sovereignty in the earth.

Translation: He's already showing off.

Our Lord Jesus provided a litany of signs that would manifest near the end of the dispensation of man. The first stage of these signs includes war, rumors of wars, famines and earthquakes in diverse places (Mt. 24:4-8, Mk. 13:5-8). Sounds like today's news cycle, literally, today. Verse 8 indicates that these signs are the beginning of sorrow. One translation (NIV) says these signs are the beginning of birth pains, which is the meaning of the original Greek word.

Well, what's about to be born? Glory. Glory returning. Glory rising. I submit that it is the Glory of God covering the earth as the waters cover the sea.

There are at least four manifestations of Glory rising that are already happening in the earth today: (1) Global Warning, (2) False Doctrine, (3) Evil Exposed, and (4) Fearful Hypocrites.

**(1) Global Warning** (unusual climate patterns; more violent earthquakes). Climate change has been catapulted to the front and center of policy and economical discourse. Global warming is resisted by some, but *global warning* is undeniable. Super-storms, devastating hurricanes, riveting earthquakes and tsunamis all portend the sky and the earth being shaken. The earth responds to its Creator. The earth trembles and quakes at the Lord's approach.

This brings to mind the occasion when God gave the Ten Commandments to Moses at the top of Mount Sinai. While God spoke to Moses in the thick cloud, Exodus 20:18 records '...*all the people saw the thunderings, and the lightnings, and the noise of the trumpet, and the mountain smoking: and when the people saw it, they removed [from the base of the mountain], and stood afar off'.' (KJV)*

God speaks forth His statutes like a trumpet on the mountain—
and the mountain smokes and experiences its own *personal
weather system!*

So, as was already discussed in a previous chapter, changes in weather patterns, especially the increase in earthquakes are definitely signs of Glory Rising.

**(2) False Doctrine**. Jesus warned us that false teachers would arise (Mt. 24:11), and they have arrived in full force. We have already mentioned the erroneous 'all blessing no trial' teaching, but there are so many others, including cults, pagan religion, witchcraft, *etc,*

But there exists a falsehood even worse than these types. A false teacher is not only one who teaches the Bible in error, but also one who may deliver the Word of God accurately but willingly lives his or her life in error and debauchery. Such leaders have no intention of practicing what they preach.

These are the worst sorts of false teachers: double-minded, of necessity sneaky to maintain their virtuous image in public; accomplished in hypocrisy. Their words are correct on the surface, but they are saturated with whatever evil is cherished by that speaker. The recipient, the audience with an open heart, *haplessly drinks*.

And the evil or evil *complacency* becomes
fruitful and multiplies.

The Pharisees and scribes were the false teachers during Jesus' earthly ministry, The Lord exposed their hypocrisy when He advised the people to carefully do what the Pharisees said but to absolutely avoid how they lived (Mt. 23:3).

So, why this proliferation in false teachers (and false prophets)?

The short answer is that the enemy *satan* must try to distract from the real message, from the Gospel of Jesus Christ that absolutely saves. The devil knows that God's truth can and will destroy all his lies. On the other hand, he also knows that the world (and sadly, quite a few in the Church) love being entertained. Thus, satan is counting on soothing false teachings and spectacular false miracles to turn droves of people away from Christ.

Just as the Egyptian priests were able to imitate the first few signs that Moses demonstrated before Pharaoh,[65] so satan, the father of lies, would dare try to imitate Glory rising with a few spectacular feats of his own—the Bible calls them *lying wonders*.[66]

God's Glory is rising; the devil is being backed against the wall. His time is short so, like a cornered animal, he's going to lash out. He's got to bring out the big guns: rulers of darkness and spiritual wickedness in high places (Eph. 6:12). That ol' devil isn't about to play fair. He's the father of lies and he's going to deploy his arsenal of lies. He's going for broke. So if we don't rely on the discernment of the Holy Spirit, *even the elect, those who are born again will be fooled*[67].

Please don't be deceived about how easily humans can be deceived, even Christians. Nobody can handle this new wave of satanic deception without clinging to Christ *and* resolving to obey Him. This is the time to draw closer to the Lord so that we are absolutely familiar with His voice and know how to run—correction, *flee* from the voice of a stranger.

**(3) Evil Exposed**. Another manifestation of Glory rising may seem counterintuitive at first. Sometimes a scandal breaks in an organization, or there's one news report after another of the same type of wrongdoing. We may hearken to the civil rights era when the evening news showed visceral images of marchers being hosed down and dogs attacking some of them.

Similarly today, people hear a rash of similar stories and shake their heads, concluding that such and such problem is a new terrible development, when in fact the problem has been around all along; it's just now being exposed. Ephesians 5:13 says: *But all things that are reproved are made manifest by light: for whatever makes manifest is light.* Another translation is even more direct: *But their evil intentions will be exposed when the light shines on them, for the light makes everything visible.*[68]

So when the same issue keeps appearing in the news cycle, it's not because evil prevails, and will always be that way but, rather, because the evil that had indeed been prevalent in the past is finally being exposed, so that it may be judged.

When one considers the tragedy that took place in Mother Emanuel AME Church in Charleston, South Carolina, followed by the amazing forgiveness of all the families toward the shooter, the outpouring of love and coming together of South Carolinians of all stripes, and the state's decision to remove the Confederate flag from the Capitol grounds—that's an example of Glory taking territory.[69] That is the kind of definitive outcome that only Jesus' love can catalyze.

Whatever is the issue to which you are drawn, that catches your eye or ear in the media, that is probably the Holy Spirit prompting you to pray and to act on behalf of that issue. Pray for your city or town, pray for children and family, pray for our politicians, our soldiers and veterans, and for missions here and abroad. Identify your assignment, the issue or institution for which God has created you to spur change. Pray *and take godly action* until the resident evil in that situation is exposed, uprooted and God's mercy takes over.

**(4) Fearful Hypocrites**. Well, now we're back to talking about Glory in the church house, because that's where these types of hypocrites to which God is referring breed. When the Glory of God does manifest, it doesn't fare so well for them. Isaiah 33:14 spells it out plainly:

*The sinners in Zion are afraid; fearfulness hath surprised the hypocrites. Who among us shall dwell with the devouring fire? who among us shall dwell with everlasting burnings? (NLT)*

Note that Zion or Mount Zion represents the place where God dwells and where He communes with His people. It is still used today to refer to the nation of Israel or to Jewish nationalism. In the New Testament, Zion is a type for the mature Body of Christ, the Church that embraces Its Glory-assignment. Hebrews 12:22 exhorts believers: '*But you have come to Mount Zion, to the city of the living God, the heavenly Jerusalem...' (NIV)*

Returning to Isaiah 33, the backdrop is this: the entire army of Assyria had just been demolished by one angel sent from God. One single, *nameless* angel had slain 185,000 enemy soldiers in one night. Twenty-four hours ago, King Hezekiah and Israel were afraid of King Sennacherib of Assyria. Twenty-four hours later, they're much more afraid of the God of Israel. *Especially the hypocrites.*

There is good fear and there is bad fear. It was good that Israel— seeing their previously besieged city now surrounded by *piles of corpses*—had seared into their conscience a *crystallizing* picture of Jehovah's sovereignty. But that same spectacle terrified those Jews who, by their unwavering allegiance to their secret debaucheries, had dismissed God as one big joke. Apparently, HE WAS NOT.

It's the same today. When the glory of God really comes through a service, and people are in intense worship, nobody is more discombobulated than hypocrites, who have grown comfortable with God being far away. The entire Church is rejoicing at the powerful way that God has manifested among them, but a few folk look worried instead. That's because they had no control over what just took place or they never could have predicted what just took place. *That* wasn't supposed to happen! If God can do all that, that means that He knows about my….

*Lightning that struck that close to home might find its target on the next strike.*

Nearly 300 years ago, the theologian Matthew Henry had this to say about church hypocrites:

*There are sinners in Zion, hypocrites, that enjoy Zion's privileges and concur in Zion's services, but their hearts are not right in the sight of God; they keep up secret haunts of sin under the cloak of a visible profession, which convicts them of hypocrisy. Sinners in Zion will have a great deal to answer for above other sinners…always subject to secret frights and terrors…struck with a more than ordinary consternation from the convictions of their own consciences.*[70]

It seemed that the venerable clergyman had also witnessed the paranoia that characterizes those believers who chose their pet vice over the impassioned pursuit of Christ.

One thing is for sure: as surely as God lives, the Glory of God is coming. The Glory of the Lord is rising upon His Church. The earth in anticipation is already quaking. The wrongs are going to be righted and the nonsense is going to be judged. Ready or not,

*Glory is going global.*

**Let's pray.**

Lord help us! Help us to understand and to respect Your Glory, for this is not the time to play. This is not the time to waver in the faith. Help us to not be afraid, but to be aware of what You are doing in the affairs of men. Lord, deliver us from evil and steer us from deception. Teach us how to discern the news, and all that we hear, by the Holy Spirit, and not be taught a secular conclusion by the media.

Lord we know that You commanded us to be holy as You are holy, just as You commanded Lazarus to come forth from the grave. Just like Lazarus, we can't <u>do</u> <u>it</u> without You. It takes Your Glory to be raised from dead works, to be transformed into Your likeness, to be radical for Christ and not burn out. If we're going to keep growing from glory to glory, Glory, not hype, must fuel our journey.

We are tired, O King, of being timid. We are tired, O King, of being ordinary. We are ready to walk in the extraordinary. We are ready to advance and gain territory. Show us Your Glory and make us the vessels of deliverance and graciousness that You have already ordained us to be. Show us how to exalt Jesus in the earth. Show Your wonders, Your judgments and most of all, Your goodness. Let all of the earth be full of Your Glory, O King of kings!

And joyfully, we give You all the praise, for we live to Give God Great Glory—

In Jesus' Name—Amen!

# 14

# PARTING WORDS: IT ALL COMES DOWN TO THIS

*After these things the word of the Lord came unto Abram in a vision, saying, Fear not, Abram: I am thy shield, and thy exceeding great reward. Gen. 15:1 (KJV)*

My dear friend, now, that we have come to the end, I hope that for you it is just the beginning. I pray that you have been transformed and empowered by God's strong presence as you read the pages of this book. I pray that your heart is racing with new heavenly ideas, with sure confirmation of why such and such happened in your life, with crystal clear affirmation of your divine assignment. I deeply hope that you are acutely aware of God's delight in you and of God's Glory rising in your life.

Now the Holy Spirit will take things from here, leading and guiding you into all truth. As a collaborator with Christ, you have been summoned to a grand and holy adventure. Your story is uniquely your story, but I can predict how this wondrous adventure will end, for its glorious *overarching* narrative has been repeated innumerable times:

A new babe in Christ starts his or her journey with God in anticipation of earthly conquest and heavenly reward. That is how it should be. Developing faith is the key, for without faith it is impossible to please God.[71] The new Christian is motivated to be strong in faith, for God promised to be the Rewarder of those who diligently seek Him. So he or she diligently seeks God for the Reward.

*For the Lord God is a sun and shield: the Lord will give grace and glory: no good thing will he withhold from them that walk uprightly. Ps. 84:11 (KJV)*

As the Christian grows, some who started with him or her turn away. They get sidetracked, caught up with lesser rewards of riches, power, fame or pleasure.  Unwisely, they substitute the pursuit of God with the pursuit of happiness. The Christian sadly parts with this friend, then that relative, just as Abram had to part with his nephew Lot[72]. We still love them, but we've been called by Christ on a journey to Glory to which we must respond.

The Christian continues to seek God, desiring the exceeding riches that God has promised.  He or she experiences more victories in spite of more persecution. He or she continued to be glorified, to be transformed by the renewal of the mind. The Glory continues to rise upon this Christian until a marvelous epiphany occurs: she or he ultimately learns that the *reward of the journey is God Himself.*

The One who started you *on* the journey, and never abandoned you *in* the journey is the whole point *of* the journey.  It all comes down to this:

**God Himself is our exceeding great reward**.

Thus, Glory has accomplished its finest work in our lives when we finally value that we already have access to the King of kings and the Lord of lords—God, our *exceeding great reward* as well as our *exceeding great Savior.*

The journey to Glory has fitted us for Glory, that we may realize the prayer of Jesus: become one with God, sworn to His good purpose, and find all of our satisfaction in Him. There is no limit to what you and I can accomplish, or what territory can be gained for Christ, once we get ourselves out of the way and let God's Glory rise in us.

It all comes down to this:

Somebody in this world is desperate, longing to see Christ in you. **Go!**

---

*For Thine is the kingdom, the power and the glory, now and forever, Amen.*

---

*It took me eighteen years to produce my first book. It took me forty days to produce this current book. I believe that Glory was wondrously at work.*

I give all glory to the Lord Jesus who saw fit to call me to His purposes. I also owe a debt of gratefulness to the many remarkable people that have contributed to the realization of **Glory Rising**. The posture of my faith is in large part due to the prayers, sermons, encouragement, critique, integrity, innovation, fellowship, humor, collaboration, sacrifice, intercessions, prophecy, strength and faith that others have shared with me. I am grateful for their godly impartation into my life.[73]

I thank my parents William and Dr. Bettye Greene (both deceased), who prayed for me, trained me, invested a lot of money in me, and always expected greatness from me (even when I didn't expect it from myself). There's simply not adequate space to chronicle their enduring sacrifices. I only hope that I make them proud.

Thanks to my husband Arnold of thirty years, and our son Jeremy for putting up with and praying for me! Arnold is my best friend, sounding board, AR, and stylist. He makes me look gorgeous and challenges me to be spiritually effective. He is definitely the right Adam for this Eve. My son Jeremy encourages me with percipient insight, given his age. He turned out to be a very accomplished young man. He blesses me in ways of which he is not even aware.

I cherish my spiritual training under Bishop Arthur M. Brazier, my pastor for 29 years. I did not inherit his eloquence, but hopefully his integrity and his passion for souls to be saved. What boldness presents itself in my writings I have derived from his profound example. In my ministry, I try to 'get to the Cross as fast as I can'. Bishop is in heaven, but I remember, rehearse, and treasure his lessons.

Thanks to Dr. Jeanne Porter King for her sage encouragement and for her consistent excellence in ministry; to Minister Leola Stuttley Bell—for her passion and for powerful strategies in prayer; to Dr. Jacqueline Anderson for her boldness, and brilliance coupled with rare humility that has inspired me; to the witty Evangelist Kay Robinson for her friendship and editorial insight through the years. Thanks to Reverend Eugene and Yolanda Blair, who profoundly understand and revere the Glory of God.

Thanks to Julie Gordon for her critical reading of this manuscript and the essential fact-checking. Thanks to Sis. Kitty Daily, for her incisive critique as well as her superb administrative skills. I am also grateful for long conversations with my upbeat friend and gifted artist Minnie Watkins. I deeply appreciate the encouragement, advice, integrity and well-honed spiritual discernment of all these gifted women.

Thank you Lord Jesus, for new mercies daily, for replacing my sorrow with gladness, for purposing my life, and for the heart-throbbing wonder of Your Glory Rising.

1    Birds reference: *2,000 geese fall dead 'out of the sky' in Idaho.*
     USA Today. March 18, 2015. Accessed July 23, 2015. http://
     www.usatoday.com/story/news/nation/2015/03/17/
     snow-geese- dead-idaho/24898081/

     Phil Vinter. *Scientists Baffled As Thousands Of Dead Fish
     And Birds Wash Up On Shore Of Lake Erie* DailyMail.com.
     September 6, 2012. Accessed July 23, 2015. http://www.
     dailymail.co.uk/news/article-2199471/Scientists-baffled-
     thousands-dead-fish-wash-shore- Lake-Erie.html

     Gun violence reference: *After Years of Declining Crime,
     a Spike in City Violence.* ABC News Chicago. Jul 11,
     2015. Associated Press. http://abcnews.go.com/US/
     wireStory/years-declining- crime-spike-city-violence-
     32382268?singlePage=true

     Weather reference: Richard Haugh. *East Coast Storm Surge:
     What Happened Next?* BBC News. 5 December 2014. http://
     www.bbc.com/news/uk-england-norfolk-30183045

     Melanie Fitzpatrick and Erika Spanger-Siegfried. *East Coast,
     Gulf Coast Should Get Used To Tidal Floods.* CNN. October
     21, 2014. http://www.cnn.com/2014/10/21/opinion/
     fitzpatrick-east-coast- flooding/

     Ben Tracy. Record *West Coast Drought Shows No Signs Of
     Easing.* CBS News. February 20, 2015. http://www.cbsnews.
     com/news/record-west-coast-drought-shows-no-signs-of-
     easing/

     Andrea Rumbaugh. *Insurers Cite Tough Texas Weather As
     Homeowner Premiums Rise.* Houston Chronicle. September 17,
     2014

     Marc Jones. *The Insurance Industry Responds To Climate Change*

*Risk*. Risk Management Magazine. February 2, 2015. http://
www.rmmagazine.com/2015/02/02/threat-level-rising-the-
insurance-industry-responds-to-climate-change-risk/

Mean-spiritedness reference: AnneClaire Stapleton and
Steve Almasy. *ESPN Reporter Britt McHenry Suspended
After Berating Towing Company Clerk*. CNN. April 20, 2015.
http://www.cnn.com/2015/04/16/us/espn-reporter-britt-
mchenry-tirade/

Joseph Diaz, Lauren Pearle and Alexa Valiente. *What Life in
Captivity Was Like for Cleveland Kidnapping Survivors Amanda
Berry and Gina DeJesus*. ABC. Apr 27, 2015. http://abcnews.
go.com/US/life-captivity-cleveland-kidnapping-survivors-
amanda-berry- gina/story?id=30532737

Identity reference: Dana Ford and Greg Botelho. *Who Is
Rachel Dolezal?* CNN. June 17, 2015 http://www.cnn.
com/2015/06/16/us/rachel-dolezal/

Jacque Wilson. *5 Things To Know About Gender Identity*. CNN.
August 23, 2013. http://www.cnn.com/2013/08/22/health/
bradley-manning-gender-identity/

Cyber terrorism reference: David Goldman and Jose
Pagliery. *New York Cinema Cancels "The Interview" Premiere
After Hackers' Threat*. CNNMoney. New York. December 29,
2014.

David Goldman. *Hacker Hits On U.S. Power And Nuclear
Targets Spiked In 2012*. CNN Money (New York). January 9,
2013.

All online references accessed July 23, 2015

² KJV

[3]    http://god.net/god/articles/the-glory-of-god/

[4]    2 Cor. 3:18 (KJV): *But we all, with open face beholding as in a glass the glory of the Lord, are changed into the same image from glory to glory, even as by the Spirit of the Lord.*

[5]    Particularly in physics! For instance, there's the adage 'moving charges cause light'. That is not quite correct, it's not enough to be moving, accelerating charges cause light according to James Clerk Maxwell. You can't be 'the light of the world' (Mt. 5:14) without being charged up, you can't be laconic about it, you've got to be excited about Jesus, charged with His mission to go change the world—but you can't move at last year's pace and generate this year's light. You've got to be moving more intentionally in God as time progresses. In other words *only if one is improving, exceeding, multiplying does one continue to produce spiritual light.*

And another thing about light, the speed of light itself is a constant (an invariant), meaning any measurement in an inertial frame from anywhere in the world will give the same value for the speed of light whether the measuring device was stationery or moving. There is relativity in time and space, but light's *speed* is an absolute value. This essential quality of light, its speed, is a constant ~three hundred million meter per second. Well, God is light, He's absolute and He changes not. No matter how, where, or when you observe Him: if the assessments are unbiased, all will arrive at the same conclusion.

There are SO many more amazing one to one physics analogies! How about in your vocation? There is no speech or language where God's voice is not heard.

[6]    1 Cor. 12:21

[7]    1 John 5:4

8    http://www.aavso.org/vsots_alphaori American
     Association of Variable Star Observers

9    Gen. 1:26, Ecc. 3:11, Ps. 139:14

10   Mt. 6:11, Lk. 11:3

11   http://www.physics.org/facts/sand-galaxies.asp

12   There are about as many stars in the universe as there are
     atoms in one gram of hydrogen.

13   A principle that Sarah might have done well to apply,
     instead of trying to help God out with 'Hagar can stand in
     proxy for me' suggestion (Gen. 16).

14   http://www.universetoday.com/18028/sun-orbit/

15   Ps.147:4

16   Hobby-Eberly Telescope Dark Energy Experiment
     http://hetdex.org/dark_energy/dark_matter.php also
     NASA: http://science.nasa.gov/astrophysics/focus-areas/
     what-is-dark-energy/ About 73 percent of the mass and
     energy in the universe is due to dark energy, while another
     23 percent is due to dark matter. Thus only about 4 percent
     of the universe is composed of regular matter and energy.
     Dark matter was suspected by Fritz Zwicky in 1933 to
     account for 'missing' mass clustered galaxies as they orbited.
     Dark energy was independently discovered by Adam Riess
     and Saul Perlmutter in late 1997.

17   Ez. 28:14

18   Is. Ch. 14

19   The word translated the angels is *Elohim* so in other Bible
     versions, the phrase becomes 'Yet you have made him a little
     lower than God...' ( for example, NASV)

[20] Php. 3:19.

[21] Gen. 6:5, and, unfortunately, *déjà vu* Tim. 3:13

[22] Heb. 3:7-16 the account of Numbers 13, 14 is retold in Hebrews 3 and 4 because God is just as adamant today that His people be people of faithfulness who are eager to believe His promises.

[23] There are five major covenants (some schools suggest more): Noahic Covenant (Gen. 9:1-15), Abrahamic Covenant. (Gen 12:1, 17:2), Mosaic Covenant (Ex. 24:3-8,Ten Commandments Ex. 20:1-17) Davidic Covenant (2 Sam. 7:12-13; Rev. 22:16); Covenant of Christ that secured salvation (Heb. 8:15-28, Heb. 10:19-24).

[24] Also Mk. 8:35, Lk. 9:24

[25] BBC http://www.bbc.com/news/blogs-news-from-elsewhere-28034240; Last Week *Tonight with John Oliver:* https://www.youtube.com/watch?v=D_GzHyEWkJY; New York Post http://nypost.com/2014/06/27/boko-haram-insurgents-arrested-after-fleeing-bees- and-snakes/

[26] Mt. 24:7, Mk. 13:8, Lk. 21:11

[27] Tsunamis are most commonly generated by earthquakes in marine and coastal regions. http://www.tsunami.noaa.gov/tsunami_story.html

[28] 1 Sam. 31:2, 6 : Jonathan, Abinadab, and Malchishua

[29] 1 Sam. 10:11

[30] If you read the entire account, Saul side-stepped Samuel at first. His first answer 'Yes I did obey God in the way He instructed. But the people took the best of the livestock.' (1

Sa. 15:20-21) This is a contradiction. If you obeyed God, how could the word "but" follow?

[31] threw javelin at David twice to kill him; 1 Sam 18:10-11, threw a javelin at his son Jonathan,19:9- 10, 19:30-32 ; had 85 members of Abiathar's family (Ahimelek the father) killed for 'assisting' David. 22:6-19

[32] ibid

[33] 1 Sam. 28:7

[34] 2 Sam. 3:1

[35] http://www.bible.ca/archeology/bible-archeology-exodus-route-wilderness-of-sinai.htm

[36] Is. 53:6

[37] Ex. 32:27-28, 35

[38] Character also sources 'the things that do appear' (Heb. 11:3). God saw that every thing He had was very good (Gen. 1:31). Every good and perfect gift is from God (James 1:17).

[39] *Grace Greater than Our Sin* Julia H. Johnston written in 1910

[40] Salvation and glory flow together: *In God is my salvation and my glory: the rock of my strength, and my refuge, is in God.* Ps. 62:7

[41] 1 Chr. 4:10 referred to as the prayer of Jabez

[42] Eph. 3:18

[43] One of Bishop A. M. Brazier's regular monikers for the prophet Isaiah.

44 Mt. 1:17

45 Gal. 3:29

46 In light of the civil conflict that has lately befallen our great country. I believe that when wickedness is exposed and all flesh sees it together on CNN, on the internet, in the news cycle,

47 God's Glory is at work. As Glory rises, wrong is exposed and eventually judged. Romans 8:28 And we know that all things work together for the good for those who love God and are called according to His purpose,

48 *Amazing.* Think of all the mistakes—often repeated— foolish decisions, hasty words, regrets. But now, if we only determine to spend our remaining days wisely, to obey Jesus and refuse to waver, God can still assure us eternal victory *as if no time had been wasted*—(which it has!)

49 He that descended is the same also that ascended up far above all heavens, that he might fill all things. Eph. 4:10 (KJV)

50 Rom. 6:4

51 1 John 2:16

52 Col. 2:9

53 Through a dream the Holy Spirit released the apostle Peter to preach Christ to the Roman centurion Cornelius (Acts Chapter 10 )

54 Ruth, Esther, Daniel, and others could have also been included.

55    It is also interesting in passing to note that one of these
      individuals could already speak several languages to
      carry out his glory-assignment while the other three *had
      to learn another language/culture* to accomplish their glory-
      assignments. Hint.

56    I sometimes imagine that God placed Paul in Damascus
      on purpose so that he could witness that, absent Christ,
      there wasn't a lot of moral difference between Jews and the
      inhabitants of Damascus. The lack of mercy was running
      neck and neck. (Islam would be established in Damascus
      about 600 years later).

57    Quency E. Wallace. Early Life and Background of Paul
      the Apostle. (2002) Accessed Aug 1, 2015. http://www.
      biblicaltheology.com/Research/WallaceQ01.html
      Paul's powerful intellect was informed by his unique
      upbringing as both Jewish elite and Roman citizen in the
      renowned academic city of Tarsus. He deeply understood
      the psyche of the Jew and of the Gentile (1 Cor. 12:22-24).
      Now all that remained was for him to learn the mind of
      Christ.

58    Is. 58:12

59    The *Lilium regale* is plant hunter Ernest H.
      Wilson's most famous introduction, both for its beauty
      and for nearly costing him his life http://www.pbs.org/
      wgbh/nova/flower/gard-nf.html

60    Most theologians ascribe the phrase in Song of Solomon 2:1
      as describing Christ.

61    Song of Solomon 2:2, 2:16 and 6:31: 'feeding among the
      lilies'—the lily patch or field is where Christ may be found,
      so if you search for Christ, that's where you'll find more

truth about Him...more precisely, if the search is intentional and desperate enough that's when you'll find more truth about Him.

[62] Charles H. Spurgeon. Sermon 994, 'The Prayer of Jabez'. (1871). Newington, England. Accessed July 30, 2015 http://www.spurgeon.org/sermons/0994.htm

[63] 2 Cor.12:9-10. Truth in disclosure: there is also the opportunity to become bitter, but I pray that we opt out of that choice.

[64] Sometimes called cloud to air (CA) or cloud-to-cloud lightning. http://www.nssl.noaa.gov/education/svrwx101/lightning/types/

[65] Ex. 7:11, 22, 8:18-19

[66] 2 Thess. 2:9, though many theologians believe that this scripture specifically speaks to the end- stage of the end times, there are false ministers operating contemporaneously; the concept of lying wonders—wonders that support a lie—are not just for the 'by and by'—see Deut. 13:1-4

[67] (Mt. 24:11,24) Note: I did not say *be lost,* I said *be fooled.* Even now there are some truly born again, good saints faithfully sending monthly checks to support the ministries of charlatans and spiritual baboons.

[68] NLT 69 http://www.cnn.com/2015/07/12/us/charleston-south-carolina-emanuel-ame-church-new-chapter/

[70] https://www.blueletterbible.org/Comm/mhc/Isa/Isa_033.cfm

[71] Heb. 11:6

[72] Gen. 13:14

[73] Thanks to Precious, Lenora, Julie, Shauntia, Chris, Robin, Rachel, Jolande, Travis, Requitta, Billy, Joe Mac, Percy, Cynthia, David, Millicent, Steve, Candy: dear friends, fellow ministers and awesome psalmists!

Made in the USA
Lexington, KY
01 October 2016